Library of
Davidson College

SCHOLARSHIP AND ITS SURVIVAL

A CARNEGIE FOUNDATION ESSAY

SCHOLARSHIP AND ITS SURVIVAL

QUESTIONS ON THE IDEA OF GRADUATE EDUCATION

JAROSLAV PELIKAN

THE CARNEGIE FOUNDATION
FOR THE ADVANCEMENT
OF TEACHING

5 Ivy Lane
Princeton, New Jersey 08540

Copyright © 1983
The Carnegie Foundation
for the Advancement of Teaching

This essay is published as part of an effort by The Carnegie Foundation for the Advancement of Teaching to explore significant issues in education. The views expressed should not necessarily be ascribed to the Board of Trustees of the Foundation or to its individual members.

Copyright under International Pan American and Universal Copyright Conventions. All rights reserved. No part of this book may be reproduced in any form—except for brief quotation (not to exceed 1000 words) in a review or professional work—without permission in writing from the publisher.

LIBRARY OF CONGRESS CATALOGING IN PUBLICATION DATA
Main entry under title:
Scholarship and its Survival
   Includes bibliographical references.
   1. Universities and colleges—United States—Graduate work. I. Title.
LB2371.P394   1983   378'.1553'0973   83-15211
ISBN 0-931050-24-3

Copies are available from the
PRINCETON UNIVERSITY PRESS
3175 Princeton Pike
Lawrenceville, N.J. 08648

To my *Doktorvater*
WILHELM PAUCK
(1901-1981)

CONTENTS

Foreword
by Ernest L. Boyer
ix

Preface
xvii

Whither Graduate Education?
1

I. College into University?
5

II. A Lost Generation of Scholars?
15

III. A Gentleman—and a Scholar?
25

IV. Knowledge or Professional Skill?
41

V. Beyond Competence: Integrity?
53

VI. Elitism Versus Egalitarianism?
67

Appendix
79

Notes
85

Index
95

FOREWORD

IF ANYTHING IS CLEAR from the debate on education in America, it is that the various levels of formal learning cannot operate in isolation. It is a mistake to talk about the reform of the high school without relating that institution on the one side to elementary education and on the other to higher education. It is a mistake to deal with college or so-called undergraduate reform without making the connection between undergraduate and graduate education. Graduate education cannot be improved in isolation from the neighbors without whom it cannot live, let alone prosper. Graduate education connects to the undergraduate college and to the professional schools.

This obvious truth obviously has been violated. Under the twin banners of professionalism and specialization, the formal branches of teaching and learning have tried to go it alone. Not until something (say, the absence of basic skills in students) stopped them in their tracks, have educators bothered to take notice of each other—too often in an accusatory or denunciatory way. High school students cannot read and write. Why? Because of deficiencies in the elementary school (where the responsibility for the problem is transferred along to the student's home). College students do not measure up. Why? Because the high schools have failed (or perhaps because the colleges have given poor guidance to the high schools).

The ultimate humiliation comes when students in graduate school cannot read, write, compute, or communicate at a level of skill sufficient to the demands of advanced education. Is the blame to be put on the college out of which they come or on professional and career programs where the education may be as narrow as the student's ignorance outside the specialization is wide?

Clearly, we are in the soup together. No one should be denied a share of the blame. But, also, no one is without resources for effecting a remedy.

Because education is indivisible, The Carnegie Foundation has organized its policy studies around the connections between educational institutions and the various levels of education.

Thus, in recent years we have looked at the high school, the school-college connection, general education programs in the college, the connection of higher education to the state, and the upper division years of the undergraduate curriculum (which will be the subject of an essay to be published soon). Our aim is to show that the education pieces taken separately have a restricted meaning but, put together, reveal a larger picture. The *whole* can, we argue, be greater than the sum of the parts.

It is appropriate, and perhaps mandatory, therefore, that the Foundation give special attention to graduate education in America. In this case, our decision was to commission an essay to a distinguished scholar with experience in graduate school administration. That call went to Jaroslav Pelikan, Sterling Professor of History and former dean of the graduate school at Yale University. This book is the result of that commission.

Professor Pelikan's questions in this essay raise again the issue of vital connections—the graduate school in connection with the college as well as with professional schools, the graduate program revised to assure that balance in these connections is achieved even as integrity in all phases of the work must be preserved.

Pelikan argues persuasively that graduate education is

something special and, therefore, has something uniquely important to bring to students and to other institutions that are in connection with graduate schools. That something special is scholarship.

In American education there are what we call "basic skills." There also are advanced skills. There is general education, but also there is specific education that involves knowing one subject very well. There are applied fields of teaching and learning; also there are theoretical studies. There are ideas. There is action. There is reason to be concerned about the better use of existing knowledge and available information. But there is also need for new knowledge, for work on what academics call "the growing edge of knowledge." This latter task is the established responsibility of research and scholarship. And the graduate school is its home.

Graduate schools, as Professor Pelikan says, are places where academic scholarship should prosper. But his essay suggests that it is no longer certain that scholarship is at home in graduate schools or that graduate education is a true expression of scholarship.

"The graduate school," he says, "finds itself cast in the role of the university's bureau of standards." And what are some of the standards that are more important than others, perhaps most important of all?

First, "scholarly research defines the nature of the university" according to Pelikan, and it is scholarly research that makes the difference between the university and a college in America. This fact, and the prospect that the ranks of university scholars will continue to thin out under pressures from competing professions and a paucity of opportunity for young scholars, makes it imperative that demographic realities and their implications for the future be a part of any discussion of "scholarship and its survival." Dr. Pelikan warns that the vitality and growth of scholarship is threatened now because there are too few new recruits in the ranks of the scholars. As

David Riesman put it, the nation must protect its seed corn.

In addition to attracting good students, universities must improve general education if scholarship is to survive as the cornerstone of graduate schools. Pelikan writes: "the quality of scholarship is itself bound up with the state, and the fate, of general education. . . ." This is the theme of continuing concern to the Carnegie Foundation.

What are the essential components of general education that, even at the graduate level, must be featured?

"At the head of the list, many scholars, regardless of field, would put the ability to use the mother tongue."

Mastery of English, careful writing, critical editing—these are among the nonnegotiable skills of scholarship. This emphasis on the centrality of language reinforces the seamless web of education. The same priority is established, for example, in the Foundation's report on American secondary education. Professor Pelikan also argues for general education with a world view. He writes that, "part of the general education of the 'gentleman' in the final decades of the twentieth century, and above all of the general education of the scholar must be a responsible acquaintance with some other culture, past or present. Ordinarily, though not necessarily, this acquaintance should include the use of its language."

One of the most surprising and important recommendations offered by Dr. Pelikan calls for more attention at the graduate level to the value of cross-disciplinary concentrations. This recommendation is a reality in the biological sciences—a prototype exists there—and the challenge now is to extend this emphasis to other areas of study.

Again, Pelikan returns to the theme of connections. Graduate schools, he argues, must coordinate their emphasis on general education with undergraduate colleges. And the college major should be considered in relation to general education and postbaccalaureate study. Here is Pelikan's audacious proposal:

. . . the case for the conventional major . . . ought to rest principally on its importance as a summation and a climax for undergraduate study rather than, as it often does now, on the foundation it supposedly lays for graduate study.

An authentic and meaningful balance, "would call for the three modalities of university education—undergraduate, graduate, and professional—to be related to one another on a divisional basis through faculty appointments and through programs of instruction and research, with each professional school related symbiotically to one (or more) of the divisions. . . ."

Viewing the college major more broadly is appropriate, says Pelikan because "as a preparation for advanced study, the major is at best ambiguous." This is so because of "the increasingly interdisciplinary character of scholarly research." Much better would be a divisional major in college leading to divisional admission to graduate school.

Balance between the graduate school and the university's professional schools also is important. Pelikan comments on "the discovery that the content of the research sponsored by the graduate school and the subject matter of the training offered by the professional school overlap considerably, and will do so increasingly." Also worth noting is the fact that professional schools, like the graduate schools, depend on the colleges to provide the general education and introduction to research as "process" more than "product" upon which advanced training depends. He adds, however, that there is not yet a corresponding integration of activities between these two important factors.

Professor Pelikan argues vigorously that much needs to be done to improve the relationship of the professional schools with the graduate school. In too many cases it appears that the professional schools are *at* the university but not *in* and *of* the university. Also, there should be a deeper appreciation for the fact that a university at its best will feature professional schools and a graduate school where attention to the advancement of "knowledge" and "training in advanced skills" go forward together.

Finally, we are reminded in this essay that if scholarship is to survive and prosper in the university, the emphasis on "balance"—between general education and advanced scholarship, between colleges and universities, between research and teaching, between graduate education and professional schools—must be equalled by an emphasis on "integrity."

There is, Professor Pelikan points out, a tendency in the university to talk glibly of the "community of scholars." But most persons engaged in such talk are "far more explicit about what 'scholars' means in that definition than about what 'community' means. . . ." It is now time for all of us to be reminded that "in the life of the university, and in the training of future scholars, community—community of labor, community of trust, but also community of integrity—is indispensable to scholarship as we know it."

In the Carnegie Foundation essay, *Higher Learning in the Nation's Service*, we made a point that lingered in our thinking and, finally, brought us to commission this essay:

> In the final analysis, research is a creative response to anything we fail to understand and yearn to know. Much of the university's future engagement with the riddles of the world will involve the flash of insight that comes only after the intellect has been disciplined in the tradition that the educator has a responsibility to pass on. Research in its purest forms is to be found in American universities, where it cannot be allowed to languish or starve. Sustaining that creative process is absolutely crucial if higher learning is to be truly "in the nation's service."

In this "little book" Pelikan avoids the quick fix, the simple bromide. Rather, with astute analyses and lucid prose he confronts us with fundamental problems about the uses of critical intelligence and points to answers that will enable scholarship to both survive and flourish. How can we, Professor Pelikan asks in the concluding chapter, pursue quality and enhance equality? Can we, at a time of reappraisal for higher education, do more with less?

Our response to Professor Pelikan's provocative questions will affect the future of the university and the nation.

PREFACE

THIS LITTLE BOOK is intended for anyone with an interest in graduate education. That means, first of all, those who have a professional responsibility for the graduate schools of American universities—presidents, deans, professors. They are the ones who will have to decide what to do about the American graduate school, which has grown over the past generation or two into the most problematical (and in many ways the most important) unit of the university.

Yet the academic professionals are not the only ones with an important stake in the future of graduate education. Each year, billions of dollars come into the graduate establishment in the form of scholarships, fellowships, research grants, and loans from public and private sources on the assumption that what goes on there is important for the cultural, scientific, technological, and even the military future of the nation. Those who bear the responsibility for the allocation of those dollars, in the Congress or in foundations or in industry, ought to understand the unique qualities of the graduate enterprise better than they often do.

Above all, however, the entire future of this vital cause depends on those relatively few in the next generation who will see in a career as scholars a mission and a vocation that they find irresistible. Because it has recently become "all but irresistible" rather than altogether irresistible, the time has come once again to make the case for scholarship as a way of life.

To put the matter quite personally for a moment, I have

often said that if I had inherited or married great wealth, I would want to be doing just what I am doing (though I might perhaps be living a little better). But, as a teacher of undergraduates in a university college, I am deeply disturbed by the question of who our scholarly posterity are to be. How can I communicate to Yale juniors and seniors the excitement and fulfillment I have found in a life of scholarship, without leading them down the road to frustration, disappointment, and tragedy?

When I retire in 1994, some of the students entering graduate school this fall will be coming up for tenure. Although in my own career I completed professional school and graduate school in the same year, I had long since decided without hesitation that scholarship, not the practice of the profession, was my vocation. But now I have come to believe, reluctantly but ineluctably, that the very survival of scholarship is at stake today.

It was this commitment to scholarship that prompted me, without any change of vocation, to agree in 1973 to serve as acting dean of the Yale Graduate School, and, in the following year, to accept an appointment as its dean, serving until 1978.

And that, quite frankly, is also why I have written this book.

Acknowledgement: I wish to express my appreciation to Lane Mann and the Carnegie Foundation staff for preparing the tables and interpretation presented in the Appendix.

WHITHER GRADUATE EDUCATION?

AMID THE CONCERN OF the general public and the outcry of political leaders on all sides about American education, we have heard comparatively little about graduate education, which receives almost no attention in *A Nation at Risk*, the most widely discussed recent review of the educational scene. At least initially, the graduate school seems to affect education in the community far less directly than does the elementary or secondary school or even the college. Only a relatively small segment of the population will ever apply to do postbaccalaureate study, particularly in the arts and sciences; at its maximum level, the number of Ph.D.s awarded in any given year amounted to something like .015 percent of the total population. Besides, it is far more difficult for those engaged in graduate education to raise such banners as "functional illiteracy" and "a rising tide of mediocrity."

Yet closer attention and more serious reflection will suggest that, in many ways, a majority of the intellectual problems of the American educational system do ultimately find their way back to the graduate school. It is, after all, the teacher of the teachers—or, sometimes, the teacher of the teachers of the teachers. Anyone who cares deeply about education and who wants to reform it must recognize that the best way of being in a position to effect any such reform is still through the agency that turns out the credentials, which is, as American education now stands, the graduate school of arts and sciences. Thus every proposal for the improvement of education at whatever level seems to involve tasks and responsibilities for which only the graduate school is equipped. And if graduate education is not in a position to undertake such tasks and responsibilities, the only alternative will be to invent another system that will be prepared to do what graduate education has been claiming to do, and perhaps has failed to do. Yet it has been the universal experience of reform movements in American higher education that those who propose to change the system must first join the union.

Despite the comparative underemphasis on graduate education in the public debates about "the crisis of American education," a small but highly competent group of scholars have been concerning themselves, especially during the past two or three decades, with the short-term and long-term implications of postbaccalaureate study in the arts and sciences. They have, on the whole, addressed their studies to policy makers, professional educators, and professional educationists, rather than, as we are seeking to do, to the broader public of all those who have a stake in graduate education, including as well university professors and prospective graduate students. Most scholars in this new field of research have been trained in applied mathematics, in demography and econometrics, and they have brought to their scholarship the highly developed methodologies of those disciplines. Daunting as some of their mathematical models may be (not to mention the solemnity of their prose about "whither graduate education?"), it is not true, as their critics may charge, that no one without an advanced grasp of calculus can make any sense at all of their analyses.

Some of the best products of such research into graduate education have helped to inform the following essay, and both the text and the notes have sought to acknowledge the debt. What follows here is in no way an attempt to duplicate, much less to supersede, the immensely valuable papers and books that have come out of the application of a quantitative methodology to the complex situation of graduate education in the America of the 1980s and 1990s. It is, rather, an effort to step back from those studies to a level of reflection that will make "the idea of graduate education" accessible to thoughtful readers who are not themselves members of the guild of econometricians and statisticians. At the same time it addresses itself to those who must concern themselves with that "idea" in very concrete terms as administrators, professors, and students. Its basic question, then, is neither "What" nor "How," but "Why."

Many of the most fundamental questions about university education, including its graduate responsibilities, are, by at least a century or so, older than any of this literature. They were raised, and sometimes also answered, by John Henry Newman's *The Idea of a University*, a book which, as George N. Shuster said, "has done more than any other to stimulate reflection on the character and the aims of higher education."[1] Alongside the indispensable quantitative analyses of graduate education in relation to economic and demographic forces, therefore, there may be a contribution to be made to the debate from the context of a scholarship in the history of ideas that can legitimately claim to stand in a direct succession from Newman's own. And as it is absolutely essential for the intellectual historian concerned about graduate education to pay attention to the work of scholars who approach it much as they might any "labor-intensive" industry, so in turn it is necessary for the intellectual historian to point out to them that the chief product of this industry is ideas, and that therefore "the idea of graduate education" and, for that matter, *The Idea of a University* must claim their attention.

I
COLLEGE INTO UNIVERSITY?

THE DIFFERENCE BETWEEN a college and a university, it has been said, is that at a university professors are paid to study: scholarly research defines the nature of the university. Yet in the opening sentence of *The Idea of a University* Newman defined the university as "a place of *teaching* universal *knowledge*," and then went on to declare: "If its object were scientific and philosophical discovery, I do not see why a University should have students."[1] Although it has become commonplace to conclude from this statement that Newman's vision of the university was cramped by an exclusive emphasis on teaching, he did in fact make scholarly research a part of the mission of the university; and in the margin of his "Rules and Regulations for the Catholic University" he even wrote: "Professors to write books."[2]

The definitive version of Newman's *Idea of a University* was published in 1873. In 1876 the Johns Hopkins University opened its doors as a full-fledged graduate university—an event that has sometimes been described as the beginning of genuine graduate education in the United States.[3] Actually, as the *Second Annual Report of the Carnegie Foundation for the Advancement of Teaching* pointed out, "the account should begin with Yale College when in 1846 graduate courses in philosophy and the arts were established and the attempt was made to superadd on the old framework of the College";[4] the first Ph.D.'s awarded in the United States were conferred there in 1861. During the decade of the founding of Johns Hopkins, the 1870s, the University of Pennsylvania, Harvard, Columbia, and Princeton, in that order, began to offer programs leading to the degree of Doctor of Philosophy.[5] Other universities soon began adding the Ph.D. to their list of degrees awarded.[6] New universities founded in the closing decades of the nineteenth century, such as the University of Chicago in 1891, made this degree the pinnacle of their academic programs, as the one degree with "a single meaning that was explicitly qualitative," since "the gist of the Ph.D. requirements was a demand for research";[7] for, in the words of William Rainey Harper, first president of the University of Chicago, "graduate work [is] the idea which has more completely controlled the policy of The University than any other."[8]

The redoubtable Benjamin Jowett, Regius Professor of Greek, Master of Balliol, and translator of Plato (who died three years after Newman), dismissed the whole notion with the exclamation: "Research! A mere excuse for idleness; it has never achieved, and will never achieve any results of the slightest value."[9] And a later professor at Oxford, best known as the author of *The Hobbit* and *The Lord of the Rings* but a notable scholar of Old English as well, expressed himself in a similar vein as late as 1966. Writing to a grandson who had become a graduate student at Oxford, he said he had always been "sceptical about 'research' of any kind as part of the occupation or training of younger people in the language-literature schools," and he attributed the growing emphasis among humanists on scholarly research to "the desire to climb on the great band-waggon of Science (or at least onto a little trailer in tow)." But for humanists, by contrast with scientists, "there is such a lot to *learn* first," and therefore graduate students in the humanities "privately desire nothing more than a chance to read more."[10] Notwithstanding such Oxonian grumblings about "research," by the time Cardinal Newman died in 1890 it was becoming an educational consensus, at least on this side of the Atlantic Ocean as well as on the other side of the English Channel, that not only (to use his words) "the diffusion and extension of knowledge," but its "advancement" as well, did belong to the essence of "the idea of a university."

Commenting on the "fantastic, disorderly diversity" of American colleges and universities as "Hotels of the Mind," Daniel J. Boorstin observed that "the tradition the Americans inherited from Europe assumed that universities were repositories of the Higher Learning, which meant, of course, the most advanced and difficult and recondite subject matters," but that in the United States "education became a curiously inverted pyramid": "if an 'opera house' in an upstart Western town would somehow bring into being the performances to justify its name, would not a 'university' also create its own constituency?"[11] In this sense, therefore, the American university, with its combination of baccalaureate "undergraduate" education and postbaccalaureate "graduate" education, was unique.

At the same time, as was pointed out by Abraham Flexner, still perhaps the sharpest analyst of American higher education in the twentieth century,[12] it is useful to see the American university as the combination, fortuitous and uneasy, of various disparate elements. Some, including its residential character, come from the British college system at Oxford and Cambridge. Others, such as the ecclesiastical auspices under which so much of American higher education has grown, are derived from the seminary system legislated by the Council of Trent in the aftermath of the Reformation and then adapted to the special needs of the "free churches" that came out of the Puritan revolution. But the graduate programs of the American university system were an import from the German universities, which were, as Joseph Ben-David has put it, "until about the 1870s . . . virtually the only institutions in the world in which a student could obtain training in how to do scientific or scholarly research."[13] After the upheavals of the First World War and the Armistice, German *Wissenschaft* continued to be committed to the ideal expressed in 1929 by one of its outstanding spokesmen, Adolf von Harnack, whom the president of the Weimar Republic had saluted a few years earlier as "the bearer of German scholarship."[14] "Never," Harnack declared, "must there be any alteration in the character of our German universities and institutions of higher learning, their dedication to teaching and research. The distinctiveness of German universities is expressed in the combination of research and teaching."[15]

Because the colonial foundations were all colleges—or perhaps more accurately collegiate seminaries, with their "core curriculum" of "rhetoric and divinity catechetical"[16]—the "superadding" of the Ph.D. to the existing baccalaureate programs set up critical tensions within the faculty of arts and sciences, which had been known in the traditional European university as the philosophical faculty. (A further confusion had its source in the practice of the descendants of two other traditional medieval faculties, theology and law, of designating the professional degree as a baccalaureate. The degrees of Bachelor of Divinity, the B.D., and Bachelor of Laws, the LL.B., continued until recent decades to be the professional degrees also for those who had already obtained the degree of Bachelor of Arts.)

Those institutions that continued to identify themselves as *colleges* rather than as *universities* and that did not aspire to offering the Ph.D. were nevertheless profoundly affected by these changes in the American university system. At many such places, including some of the best ones, it had been possible, as late as the two decades between World War I and World War II, for faculty members who had an M.A. but had never earned the Ph.D. to win tenure and to achieve the rank of full professor—and to do so with honor. A college catalog would boast that "48% of our faculty possess earned doctorates" (which, with the substitution of the J.D. for the LL.B. as the professional degree for lawyers, might sometimes include professors of political science and other fields who had graduated from law school and had not passed through the research program of the Ph.D.). All such equivocations aside, it was evident from such practices as these that the undergraduate college was under growing pressure to define its standards of intellectual and academic achievement on the basis of criteria dictated by the university, and, within the university, by the graduate school; for, to quote again from an astute foreign observer cited earlier, "intellectually the graduate school had become the decisive influence in higher education by the beginning of this century."[17] The epitome of those criteria, and the symbol of conformity to them, was the Ph.D. It was not yet a condition for an initial faculty appointment to a "ladder rank," but increasingly it would become a prerequisite for promotion to a tenured position. William James, in his article of 1903, "The Ph.D. Octopus," was expressing the misgivings of many of his contemporaries about the growing dominance of the Ph.D. in universities and now in colleges as well;[18] but, even as he published it, his own university was taking the lead in the conferral of advanced degrees in the United States. The Ph.D. was here to stay.

Yet also here in the United States the Ph.D. was, and is, a research degree for scholars, not a professional degree for teachers. As one distinguished undergraduate dean observed, the American Ph.D. "remained set to the German model" by being "directed towards research and the advancement of knowledge," despite "the fact that 90 percent of the new doctors of philosophy would enter the teaching profession, [and] that once their dissertations were accepted, most of them would never undertake further research."[19] Recent data across various disciplines appear to be simply unavailable about the latter of those observations, although an older study did indicate that, at least for historians, the number of those who went on producing scholarly work was closer to 25 percent than to 10 percent.[20] But it is the impression of several directors of major university presses that 10 percent may be quite accurate today: although the dissertation is the principal artifact produced by the Ph.D. program, in which the candidate is held to rigorous standards of research, it does not lead, in more than one case out of ten, to a lifetime of comparably rigorous scholarship. To be sure, there remains the possibility, even the probability, that the intellectual discipline represented by the dissertation will be reflected in undergraduate teaching in the form of a sense of the methods of research that will be a fundamental part of the outlook on learning communicated in college courses. Nevertheless, the dissertation is the one component of Ph.D. training for college teachers that the defenders of the status quo have found the most difficult to justify.

It is somewhat easier with other parts of the Ph.D. curriculum. Thus introductory graduate courses might communicate some of the kinds of general information about a subject that the prospective teacher of undergraduates will need, and the reading of the scholarly literature in the field that a graduate student undertakes in preparation for comprehensive examinations will certainly provide content for future college courses. Yet "the best-known academic innovation inaugurated by German-trained instructors of graduate students was the seminar."[21] American scholars who went to Germany for doctoral study during the nineteenth century repeatedly described the thrill and the terror inspired in the research seminar by the *Herr Professor* (the professor was, inevitably, a *Herr*). At its best the seminar also inspired a rigor of method that would shape the student's future research; and it became an institution: Harnack met his seminar in church history regularly for fifty-four consecutive years. Most American graduate schools, too, have developed by now an oral tradition about some of the great research seminars of past and present, in which students and faculty work together at the discipline.

When transplanted from the graduate school into the college, however, the product of this ideal of scholarly research can feel utterly bewildered. Elmer Gant must remain the most unforgettable example of such bewilderment and culture shock. As a graduate student in English at Harvard, "he had spells and rhymes of magic numbers which would enable him, he thought, to read all of the million books in the great library," which was "a furious obsession with him all the time." But when he left graduate school and began to teach college students, "he was tortured constantly by the thought of his inadequacy and ignorance" and by the "fear and trembling" with which he "approached a four-page paper" by an undergraduate.[22] Only the involuntary servitude of the undergraduate "sections" prepares a newly minted Ph.D. to do what now becomes primary for the college teacher to do in order to be successful. But what had been primary to success in the graduate program for the Ph.D. candidate is not the way to climb the ladder of success in the college faculty.

The recognition of that anomaly has led periodically to calls for the greater "professionalization" of Ph.D. training as a program of preparation for the college teacher, or for the creation of one or more alternative degrees explicitly directed to that end. One of the most thoughtful statements of that case for an alternative degree was summarized by Dressel and Thompson a decade or so after its adoption. In addition to reciting the familiar complaints about the discrepancy between a training in research and a career in teaching, they urged that the degree of Doctor of Arts would, without sacrificing intellectual quality or authentic scholarly content, be a more effective and economical way to provide professors for the nation's colleges. It could be argued as well that such a degree would be a means of restoring the Ph.D. to its true definition and of protecting it against the dilution of contents and standards that can come if its supposed significance as a research degree is adjusted to suit its actual significance as a professional degree. The publication of their proposal, however, coincided very closely with the growing awareness, to be described in Chapter 2, that there would soon be "an increasing number of Ph.D. degrees," which would cause "a surplus of terminal degree holders."[23] Similar alternatives, such as Oliver Carmichael's suggestion of a D.Phil. for college teachers as distinct from the Ph.D. for research scholars,[24] seem also, for some of the same reasons, to have been an idea whose time had not come.

There is no denying that when the graduate school's definition of scholarship does make its presence felt within the work of the college teacher, it can fundamentally distort the commitment of the undergraduate curriculum to the aims of general education. Instead of contributing to those aims, the introductory course for freshmen and sophomores becomes a recruiting ground for majors in the department and eventual Ph.D.'s, as professors seek to clone themselves and assure the future of their field. Students intent on majoring in other departments sense that they are not welcome where their technical skills, be they linguistic or quantitative, are inadequate. There is a widely held impression, justified or not, that in research-intensive universities such an attitude toward undergraduate instruction of students who will go on to concentrate elsewhere is endemic—or epidemic—in departments of science. In any case, however, the fundamental problem is a universal one, epitomizing as it does the deep cleft between the Ph.D. degree as a "trade union card" and the Ph.D. degree as a reward for scholarly research.[25]

It would, however, be a grave error to overlook the major contribution that the scholarly standards of the Ph.D. have undeniably made to the quality of undergraduate instruction in the American college. For example, by a characteristically American process of the recombinant splicing of British and German educational genes, the undergraduate seminar has become in many American colleges both a tutorial session and a specialized consideration of some text or theme. Similarly, the quality of the senior essay required of majors has unquestionably been improved by the implicit identification of the Ph.D. dissertation as the criterion for what an extended report on research ought to be. The "cloning" indulged in by professors dedicated to research, for all the danger that it may transform the college into no more than a preparatory school for graduate or professional school, has frequently been a primary force in raising the sights of professors and students and in giving them a vision of the larger world of scholarship in which an undergraduate course, no less than a graduate course, participates—or certainly should participate. As Flexner put it, "Nothing will do more to steady and improve the college itself than its assumption of such definite functions in respect to professional and other forms of special training."[26]

Among these "other forms of special training," the preparation of research scholars and scientists in the graduate schools of American universities has had a profound effect not only on the nature of undergraduate education both within those universities and in four-year liberal arts colleges, but on the quality and the content of professional education as well—a topic to which we shall return in Chapter IV. Thus Flexner's recommendation, as the first of his principles for the "reconstruction" of medical education, that "a medical school is properly a university department" and that therefore it should not try to perform its work of teaching and research in isolation from the (rest of the) university,[27] has been carried out through the affiliation of most remaining independent schools of medicine with universities.

The graduate school, then, finds itself cast—willingly or unwillingly, but often quite willingly and sometimes downright eagerly—in the role of the university's bureau of standards. That role tends to be dramatized whenever, on the basis of the criterion of scholarly publication, a junior faculty member is denied promotion to tenure: once again, in the undergraduate perception, the research demands of the Ph.D. program have taken precedence over the teaching needs of the college. The impression is widespread beyond the campus as well that, faced with the choice between teaching and scholarship, the "professoriat" will almost invariably give the nod to scholarship.[28] On the other hand, at many colleges that transformed themselves into universities by a change of academic nomenclature but not of scholarly substance, it remains true, as James B. Conant once commented, that "research and teaching are in fact completely separated because research activities among the professors are conspicuous by their absence!"[29] Whenever there have been efforts to redress the supposed imbalance, most often involving an attempt to reformulate the criteria of appointment and promotion in such a way as to give teaching equal weight with scholarship, they have reopened Newman's question of the balance between the scholarly "advancement" of knowledge through research and the "diffusion and extension" of knowledge through teaching. And that, in turn, would certainly seem to bring us back to the question of "the difference between a college and a university," with which this chapter began, as well as perhaps to the answer given there, that "scholarly research defines the nature of the university."

II

A LOST GENERATION OF SCHOLARS?

THE COMMITMENT OF the American structure of higher education to the Ph.D., both as the definition of the standard of the scholarship expected of all faculty in the college and as the highest degree awarded by the university, made it far too easy, when the opportunity arose, for academic institutions to launch new graduate programs for which they were not adequately prepared. The prestige associated with being a "university" rather than merely a "college" lured them into supposing that graduate teaching was simply a more advanced form of the advanced instruction usually offered in the final two years of college. But that supposition ignored the fundamental principle of graduate education: graduate teaching is not an extension of a professor's undergraduate teaching, but an extension of a professor's research. To become a university, therefore, a college must change its expectations about what its faculty do and about their needs in the laboratory and the library. When those who bore responsibility for higher education—administrators and professors, trustees and legislators—lost sight of that fundamental principle, the number of graduate programs grew, but the mechanisms for monitoring their quality did not.

At least by hindsight, such growth seems almost to have been inevitable, just as it seems likewise to have been inevitable that, if the opportunity were to arise, many new thousands of aspirants to higher degrees would undertake the course of study leading to the doctorate at the end of the rainbow.

Such an opportunity was provided, at the conclusion of the Second World War, by the G. I. Bill of Rights. Many who, as newly minted Ph.D.'s, began teaching during the second half of the 1940s will always remember, with a mixture of nostalgia, gratitude, and relief, what it was like to be younger than many of the students in the class and to reintroduce these young men—not very bookish perhaps, but experienced and ready to learn, with little time for nonsense—to the undergraduate studies that had been interrupted by the Selective Service system. But there was also a substantial group who had already completed their undergraduate studies before going to war. To this group the G. I. Bill represented the chance, otherwise unattainable for many of them, to go beyond college to graduate and professional study. The course of study they undertook raised the expectations of an entire generation or two of American students about graduate education—its possibilities, its prospects, and its support; the universities "graduated thousands of lawyers, doctors, engineers, teachers, managers" and thus "spawned a new, young, eager middle class."[1]

But now the eager and scholarly "middle class" is in grave danger of becoming a cynical and nonscholarly *Lumpenproletariat* instead. Between 1960 and 1974 the number of first-year graduate students in all fields (including some "professionally oriented fields") had more than trebled, increasing from 191,180 to 597,695.[2] Two books produced in the 1970s may be taken as expressive, by their very titles—*The Great American Degree Machine* and *The Overeducated American*—as well as by the data they present, of a mounting apprehension.[3] A scheme of graduate education that had managed to increase the size of its cohort of new recruits by a factor of three in the space of a mere fifteen years had clearly become a juggernaut, with a life of its own and a momentum that was getting out of control, until, as one wag suggested at the time, the number of Ph.D.'s in the land threatened to exceed the adult population.

The reasons for this explosion were multiple and complex.[4] In many of the experimental sciences, graduate students had become an indispensable supply of hands and feet for the research of principal investigators, who could neither carry on their current project nor apply for grants to support their next project without the assurance that there would be enough helots (=Ph.D. candidates) to do whatever had to be done and, not quite incidentally but of course concurrently, to fulfill the requirements of the graduate school for the degree. At best that arrangement could be a form of apprenticeship that brought the senior scientist and the junior graduate student into a genuine partnership of research unknown in other disciplines, but at worst could become a species of subtle exploitation that sacrificed the training of the graduate student as an independent researcher to the ambitions of the professor. It was made possible by the mechanism of support for scientific research developed by collaboration between the scientific community and its patrons: private foundations, for which, however, by the late 1970s, "basic research [was] . . . a declining priority";[5] and, increasingly, the federal government. Research grants would be awarded, after proper and rigorous peer review, to principal investigators, who would, in turn, undertake to support from those grants a stated number of graduate students. In some graduate schools that support would begin with the admission of those students. In others the university would agree to provide such support for the first two, three, or four semesters, until the students were ready to sign on for dissertation research that was compatible with the scientific specialty—and, of course, with the grants and projects—of the principal investigator. The whole system was, at one and the same time, a means of granting support to graduate students in the sciences and a not-so-hidden subsidy to universities, particularly to private universities, which could charge the tuition of the students against the grants.

In the humanities and some of the social sciences, graduate students were not equally necessary to the scholarly research of the professor, except perhaps to go into the library stacks to verify references in the footnotes of the next article. Instead, graduate students here (as well as in the sciences) became "section fodder," providing that indispensable third hour in a three-hour lecture course: the senior professor would hold forth to an audience of hundreds for two of the three hours, and then the graduate students (many of whom were at the same time working for the Ph.D. under the same professor) would meet the students in smaller sections to induct the young into the mysteries of the texts upon which, presumably, the professor had been basing the lectures. Compensation to graduate students for this service was, ultimately, provided by the undergraduate college, supplementing whatever stipend they were receiving from the graduate school itself. During the 1970s and 1980s, more and more graduate schools were resorting to imaginative plans of combining funds from these several sources—research grants, teaching assistantships, and graduate school fellowships—and "flattening out" the resultant sum over the four years of graduate study to provide a uniform and predictable level of support.

Thus the graduate faculty, for its own needs of both research and instruction, came to have a vital stake in the maintenance of a continuous supply of graduate students. Less obvious, but no less important, was the need for graduate students as a source of intellectual stimulation and scholarly growth. When the lottery of the admissions process in a particular year and in a particular department resulted in an entering class that was too small, the disappointment would often be expressed in the complaint, "But now I won't have enough first-year students to mount a decent seminar!" Too tight a correlation between the professor's own scholarly research and the topic of the seminar could, moreover, lead to a definition, whether of theme or of prerequisites, so specialized as to exclude graduate students from other departments and programs—students who might be, ironically, the very ones from whom would come the most exciting intellectual stimulation, for the professor as well as for the professor's "own" students.

Books like those of Adkins and Freeman expressed an alarm that had come to be shared by most other responsible observers of American higher education by the mid-1970s. At a time when the graduate school assembly lines were about to turn out 33,000 new Ph.D.'s in a single year, Allan M. Cartter, whose book, *An Assessment of Quality in Graduate Education*,[6] had helped to lay the foundations for the scientific study of graduate education, predicted that by the early 1980s there would be academic positions for only a tragically small fraction of that number.[7] Cartter brought many of his data and much of his wisdom together in 1976.[8] There were some observers who found Cartter's cassandran picture of the next decade either too grim or still not grim enough.[9] Shaken by all that they were hearing and reading, the more responsible graduate schools, in their catalogs, as well as individual departments, in their correspondence with prospective graduate students, began, as part of a policy of "truth in packaging," to issue warnings about the bleakness of the academic job market. Everyone's vocabulary seemed to have acquired the term "Ph.D. glut"—an ugly name for a reality still more ugly.

It is obvious that such warnings did not apply with equal validity to all the fields in which the Ph.D. was being offered. In clinical psychology, for example, the expectation had always been that the "doctors" would probably enter practice, combining it with research and publication, but that only a minority of them would end up as professors in colleges or universities. For this reason, the Ph.D. in clinical psychology, like that in engineering, should probably be called a "professional" degree, in the sense in which we shall be using the word in Chapter IV. According to a recent survey, just over half of those who hold the Ph.D. in chemistry are in industry, but only about a third in colleges and universities.[10] And, as is only too well known to colleges and universities currently scrambling for faculty members to meet the growing demand for instruction in computer science, the competition in that particular auction does not come chiefly from other academic institutions at all, but does appear to be coming from almost everywhere else. Thanks to the workings of supply and demand, there is less of an oversupply in some fields than in others, and none at all in a few.

Predictably, the fields in which the oversupply is the most critical belong principally to the humanities and social sciences, which have in the past placed most of their Ph.D.'s into academic positions, at least initially—according to a survey of the National Research Council of the National Academy of Sciences, more than 95 percent of those who were employed full-time in the field in which they had done their graduate study.[11] In many leading universities, these are also the departments that are among the largest and (though not automatically so) the strongest. The needs of the university's undergraduates for instruction of high academic quality in these fields had appeared to dictate as well that, if possible, there should be, in every college that had now suddenly become a university, full-scale graduate programs vertically integrated with the undergraduate offerings of such departments, to recruit and keep scholars on the faculty and (lest we forget) to supply them with teaching assistants. It is not surprising that spreading the alarm about the Ph.D. should have had its most noticeable impact here.

The starting point for any rational analysis of the present situation of graduate education, as well as for any realistic projection about the situation of the next decade or two, would appear to be one stubborn fact, obvious once stated but considerably less than obvious until stated: All the students who, for the balance of this century, could enter college at the traditional age have already been born, and there will be fewer of them for Ph.D.'s to teach than there have been. The statistics compiled and projected by the Bureau of the Census[12] indicate that the annual birth rate, which had been at about 4,300,000 in the early 1960s, has, with some fluctuation, basically declined ever since: at the end of that decade, the late 1960s, it stood at 3,500,000, and by the middle of the following decade it had gone down even further, to just over 3,100,000. On the basis of these figures, the final report of the Carnegie Council entitled *Three Thousand Futures* predicts a reduction of about one-fourth in the traditional college-age population during the final quarter of this century.[13]

The annual birth rate, regardless of what demographers or econometricians may project, can depend also on many forces deep within the society and indeed deep within the individual human psyche, that frequently transcend and defy statistical examination. Yet it is certainly with the available numbers that anyone is compelled to begin. The specific implications of those numbers for graduate education, however, are neither clear nor simple, because of what one quantitative monograph has called the "well-documented idiosyncracies of the 'academic marketplace.' "[14] Or, as another study by The Carnegie Foundation for the Advancement of Teaching has put it, "predicting future enrollments . . . is almost as hazardous as predicting the future of the college's endowment."[15] That complexity becomes evident from the comparison of two analyses of the prospects for graduate education published, recently and almost simultaneously, by two distinguished private universities with a proud record of achievement and contribution in the preparation of Ph.D.'s in all major fields. Opening with the declaration, "The single most powerful force contributing to such a sobering prognosis is demographic," one of these analyses proceeds, by a methodology that seeks to refine earlier research models, to project "a rather steady fall" of undergraduate college enrollments in the nation from a high of about 8,250,000 in 1981 to slightly more than 7,000,000 fifteen years later—thus a reduction of college students amounting to about 15 percent. The report hedges its projections with various qualifications about unpredictable factors, such as the number of students beyond traditional undergraduate age who may decide to enter college or the possibility of a surprisingly greater participation by those segments of the population, particularly the members of racial minorities, who, by necessity or by choice, have not traditionally sent their fair share of students into postsecondary study. Nevertheless, it joins itself to the cautions expressed by other studies "that wishful thinking not be allowed to shield us from harsh realities."[16]

Another such report, issued in the following year, has, after studying the same data, read them quite differently. It opens its appendix on "the reliability of enrollment projections" with the slightly tart observation: "The confidence with which demographic or econometric projections of enrollments are announced reflects the analyst's conviction that the model employed is theoretically correct and the input data reasonably accurate." While conceding that such a conviction is "often (perhaps usually) justified," the report proceeds to urge "that such predictions can be very unstable, and that predictions made as far as ten years in the future tend to be far off base." Then it goes on to argue that there is in fact not any "predictable general national pattern," and, besides, that gross national statistics are less helpful for the understanding of the prospects of any individual institution than they appear to be. "There remains the possibility," this study concludes, "that a university's own data can . . . provide sufficient information for useful predictions." On the basis of such data it projects a pattern of enrollment quite different from that contained in most of the other studies we have been citing here, and hence it recommends a bolder strategy for graduate education than the cautious policies being urged by a significant majority of the analysts of graduate education.[17]

When experts who have in common the requisite technical

skills come to such conflicting conclusions, it is, as always, difficult for laymen who lack such skills to cope with the conflict. One may be tempted to resort to an *ad hominem* (or, more precisely perhaps, an *ad universitatem*) argument by noting that the first of the two universities in the debate not only is deprived of (or, to put it another way, is free of the burden of) the range of professional schools characteristic of most of its peers, but also has only 24 percent of its students in its graduate school, while the second counts its graduate enrollment as 71 percent of its total student body.[18] This striking difference in structure could serve to account for the difference in reaction as together they contemplate the prospect of a lost generation of scholars. Yet any such explanation would, by itself, be superficial. For there is on both sides the recognition of how knotty, and indeed how capricious, the realities behind the data can be: the warning on the one hand "that these projections are rough, and it would be a mistake to invest them with specious precision," and on the other hand the concentration on the special situation of one university, predominantly graduate in its mission, which might therefore well be seen as an exception to any national trend. Unquestionably, then, the implications of demography, whatsoever they may be, for the strategy of graduate education must be an indispensable agenda item for any national debate about "scholarship and its survival."

The other statistical datum that it would be necessary to consult for any such debate is less available and even less reliable: Who is going on from college to graduate school, and, more ominously, who is not? All we seem to have is what social scientists would identify as "anecdotal evidence," but this is sufficiently troubling to merit consideration. The national press has reported that at one university that has played a leading role as a supplier of future scholars and college teachers, the news of an oversupply of Ph.D.'s and a shortage of positions is resulting in a drastic change.[19] Such press reports confirm the "anecdotal" impression of many professors about their own undergraduates, whose scholarly bent and ability would a generation ago have made them obvious applicants to some Ph.D. program somewhere. Nowadays, however, such seniors, a bit wistfully, seem to have concluded that graduate work and college teaching are a cul-de-sac. And off they go to schools of law, medicine, or business, where, chances are, they will number among their professional school classmates some of the junior faculty under whom they have been working in college, who have also been forced to give up on a career in scholarship.

At the very least, the profound differences in the implications being drawn from the same demographic data are a warning sign against the statistical reductionism that sometimes passes for scientific objectivity in the scholarly study of higher education (and not only there). The hidden power of the unexamined a prioris in such study makes it necessary that there be, in addition to the quantitative methodology, analyses of the problem that proceed from some fundamental historical and philosophical consideration. That consideration, moreover, must be the business not only of historians and philosophers, but also of those who make concrete academic decisions about graduate education. In higher education, the trite distinction between "thinkers" and "doers" is even more fatuous than it is elsewhere. Newman's *Idea of a University*, abstract though much of its discussion may sound, grew out of the very concrete task that was assigned to him of creating a new university, and it is, in that sense, the brilliant documentation of a rather miserable failure. For that very reason, however, it may serve even those who fundamentally disagree with it as the basis for the reflection that must precede responsible decision-making. Yet such reflection, in turn, requires the enlightenment and correction provided by the data and the models employed in quantitative essays on the subject.

III

A GENTLEMAN—AND A SCHOLAR?

THE CRISIS IN the graduate schools represented by the situation we have been describing in Chapter II has made it imperative to reconsider and to challenge many fundamental and all but universal assumptions. One of these, which professors often espouse in making the case for graduate work, urges that graduate education in the university is indispensable because of the contribution it makes to undergraduate education. According to this theory, the faculty time and university resources, as well as the other private and public resources, going into graduate programs provide a major, if sometimes indirect, source of strength to both the colleges that are themselves part of universities and to those whose sole mission is undergraduate teaching. If that assumption is correct, a drastic reduction in the number and size of graduate programs is bound to have a deleterious effect on undergraduate instruction. To the extent that the assumption is correct, such reduction also implies, for faculty members and administrators in colleges, a basic reconsideration of the way the intellectual life of the faculty, and of the individual professor, can be sustained and renewed. Stimulating such a reconsideration is an important subsidiary purpose of this essay.

The primary purpose of this essay is, however, to raise the question of scholarship and of its survival, which confronts a crisis of no less awesome proportions. For this question, the converse of the assumption about the link between graduate and undergraduate education is even more pertinent: the quality of scholarship is itself bound up with the state and the fate of general education, which was the theme of the first of these Carnegie Foundation essays.[1] The difference between good scholarship and great scholarship is, as often as not, the general preparation of the scholar in fields other than the field of specialization. It is general preparation that makes possible that extra leap of imagination and analogy by which scholarship moves ahead. From such studies the scholar will derive the metaphors and "paradigms" to make sense of specialized data.[2] At the same time it is necessary to ask: How much of what is done in graduate education is actually a remedial exercise to compensate for gaps, not in the preparation of students for specialized scholarship, but in their general education? To the cost of this remediation one would have to add the losses to the commonweal, quite literally incalculable, resulting from gaps in general education that will never be filled once a student has finished college, whenever universities graduate Ph.D.'s (as well as, for that matter, M.D.'s or J.D.'s) who have been well trained but poorly educated.

When John Henry Newman set about to describe the product of general education, as Culler has noted, "the term 'gentleman' could hardly be avoided altogether since it was almost a commonplace that the education of a gentleman was what the two older universities provided," but, Culler adds, "Newman did not like it." "As Newman's celebrated portrait of the 'gentleman' contains his finest comment upon the Religion of Philosophy," Culler observes later in his book, "it is ironic that this portrait should often be taken as a serious expression of Newman's positive ideal." It could not be such an expression because becoming a "gentleman" according to Newman's classic description was a necessary, but not a sufficient, result for the university to strive to produce. "At this day," Newman says in Discourse VIII, "the 'gentleman' is the creation, not of Christianity, but of civilization."[3] Only with the "apex for [the] pyramid of education," the readiness "to place [human] nature, fully developed [by general education], at the service of God," would the pyramid be complete—an ideal of which "no less than the saint is the full scope" and Saint Philip Neri the exemplar.[4]

For our purposes, however, Newman's portrait of the "gentleman" is sufficient as well as necessary, although we shall have to return to the problem of its moral and intellectual sufficiency in Chapter V. It is with that portrait that we are concerned here, more specifically with a combined portrait sketched by Robert Burns,[5] of a dog named "Caesar," whose

> letter'd, braw-brass collar
> Show'd him the *gentleman* an' *scholar*.

Beyond the satire, which is itself a healthy corrective upon the solemnity of so much educational literature, the connection (or contradiction) between the "gentleman" (regardless of gender) and the "scholar" (again regardless of gender) is pertinent to our enterprise. In that quaint phrase the term "gentleman" comes first; and it ought to, for only those young men and women who manifest the qualities of mind and spirit summarized in that term can countervail the impending catastrophe of the "lost generation." For scholars must ask themselves what they, as teachers of graduate students, wish that they and their colleagues, as teachers of undergraduates, had given them in preparation for their graduate work.

At the head of the list, many scholars, regardless of field, would put the ability to use the mother tongue. "And now abideth faith, hope, and clarity; but the greatest of these is clarity" is how some manuscripts of the English Bible read (or, at any rate, should read). Twelve or even sixteen years of school have all too often failed to inculcate a healthy respect for what Winston Churchill called "the essential structure of the normal British sentence—which is a noble thing"; he added that only for that failure would he "whip [students] hard."[6] When the products of schools and colleges are obliged to assemble a sequence of "British sentences" in some logical order into a paragraph, and a string of paragraphs into a chapter, and a group of chapters into a dissertation, they must now at last begin to learn, on graduate school time, a skill and an art that they ought to have acquired earlier and elsewhere. But the dissertation seems to be asking students to learn how to build a wall when they have not yet learned to lay brick and spread mortar. Unless the graduate schools face this issue head-on—which means more than blaming the problem on the colleges, which in turn blame it on the secondary schools, which can blame it on the elementary schools, which have no choice but to blame it on the home,[7] (all by what medieval philosophers called an "infinite regress")—much of the preparation of scholars will fail before it starts.

This implies that the universities must enforce more rigorously their requirement of the ability to write English as a prerequisite for admission to postbaccalaureate study, not alone in the humanities, but in the natural sciences and the social sciences as well (and perhaps even in the learned professions).[8] More important still is the university's enforcement of standards for written work once the student has been admitted. Long before the dissertation is due, the student must have developed habits of careful writing and critical editing. Simply reciting the usual litanies about why graduate students (and professors) cannot write is not enough. Yet many of the universities that maintain graduate programs do have at hand a resource for doing something about the problem. There are few professional cadres anywhere in the university to match the record of competence compiled by the editors on the staff of the university press. Overworked and underpaid, it is they who have often rescued distinguished scholars from the disaster of a badly written book. It would, in the long run, save money, not cost money, for those universities that have both a graduate school and a press to subsidize the appointment of additional editors at the press, so that each editor may devote part-time attention to developing the writing skills of the scholars of the next generation. And those universities that have only a graduate school and not a press could surely improvise to make free-lance editorial resources available to their graduate students (and, if one may be permitted to whisper it) to their faculty.

Consideration of the mother tongue leads directly to a discussion of other languages as a component of general education and as a requirement in graduate education. Many graduate professors could provide anecdotes to support the experience of one of their colleagues who, upon suggesting a scholarly book in French or German to Ph.D. candidates after they had passed the language examinations for the degree, has watched them "retract their 'knowledge' with an embarrassed smile."[9] Experience suggests that in any meeting of any graduate faculty, the easiest way for a professor to precipitate a controversy (or for a dean to create a diversion) is to reopen the question of language requirements for graduate degrees. The second edition of the familiar Livesey *Guide* observed in 1970 that "while the language requirement, in its various forms, remains a part of most Ph.D. programs," there was an "accelerating" trend toward its reduction or total elimination;[10] in the third edition, five years later, the very same words could appear.[11] The acceleration has continued, so that at present we appear to be in a "minimalist" period for the legislation of such requirements by the graduate schools themselves, with each individual department having something of a local autonomy to determine, perhaps with some kind of centralized review and approval, which languages, if any, are necessary for scholarly work in its discipline. These languages may range in number from none at all (in some of the natural and social sciences) to as many as six or so (in such a department as Near Eastern Languages and Literatures)—although in the latter case it is not strictly accurate to regard this as a conventional "language requirement," since several of the languages are in part the subject matter of the field rather than simply tools by which to get at the subject matter.

Even a scholar whose research has been shaped in its fundamental direction by the study of both ancient and modern languages is obliged to admit that it is possible today to do scholarly work of high quality in certain fields without being able to read any other language than English. One reason is that so many of the publications are in English to begin with; thus the director of the university presses of Norway has estimated that in Scandinavia most dissertations and monographs dealing with topics of broader than local interest appear in a world language—English above all, sometimes German or French, but not Russian or Chinese, which, for those preparing to be scholars today, must certainly qualify as *Weltsprachen*. In many fields such as physics, however, work in other languages, including Russian, Chinese, and Japanese, is being translated into English almost immediately.

A study of the history of the language requirement for the Ph.D. leads to the strong impression that it has, in any case, always been in the first instance a requirement for general education rather than for scholarly competence. How, the argument runs, could one lay claim to the title of a Doctor of Philosophy, the highest degree in the university's gift, and be illiterate in any language of culture other than one's own? But since humanists were compelled to grant that it did not seem fair to make a scientist stand examination on Leopold von Ranke or Fernand Braudel (as, of course, humanists had taken it for granted all along that their students should not have to be able to read Alexander von Humboldt or Marie Curie), the practice evolved of permitting candidates to substitute another language for the canonical two, French and German, when it could be demonstrated that the most important scholarly literature in the field was appearing, for example, in Russian. From this it followed irrefutably that if a department could show that an ability to read any foreign language at all was no longer important for scholars in its field, the requirement should be dropped. Teachers of modern languages in high school and college attribute the loss of intellectual incentive for American students to acquire another language than their own to this failure of nerve on the part of graduate schools.

Despite occasional stirrings here and there, it does not appear likely that graduate education in the United States will soon return to the earlier system of rigid and universal language requirements for the Ph.D. That makes it all the more urgent to enforce explicitly the intellectual and cultural assumptions that in fact were presupposed by that system. Part of the general education of the "gentleman" in the final decades of the twentieth century, and above all of the general education of the scholar, must be a responsible acquaintance with some other culture, past or present. Ordinarily, though not necessarily, this acquaintance should include the use of its language. The folklore of graduate students attests that it was always possible to pass the language requirements for the Ph.D. without ever having been exposed to the culture that speaks in that language. Conversely, it should be possible to acquire the perspective on one's own culture that only the study of another culture can provide without actually learning to speak or even to read its language. And for a general education, that is the least that we can require of those who want to become scholars. Whether it will also be the most that we can require would appear to depend chiefly on the colleges rather than directly on the graduate schools themselves. For if the language requirement (associated with the graduate school) is in fact a part of the general education requirement (associated with the college), it will be up to the college faculty to debate the desirability of the rule that the bachelor's degree include the mastery of a foreign language. Members of the college faculty who are at the same time graduate professors have a special responsibility to urge that the college begin to look seriously at the possibility of reintroducing the rule, for they have a special stake in seeing to it that the recipients of a bachelor's degree acquire such mastery.

A thorough consideration, however, must probably turn the usual argument by humanists in support of language requirements for the Ph.D. a full 180 degrees and raise a corollary issue: the place of quantitative skills in general education. As C. P. Snow observed in his controversial comparison of humanists and natural scientists, "the degree of incomprehension on both sides is the kind of joke which has gone sour."[12] Humanists, more than anyone else, ought to know that the prescription of the content of general education has throughout history been culturally determined. Thus Latin was part of it in the thirteenth century and Greek became part of it in the sixteenth century, but the trivium (grammar, rhetoric, and logic) and, no less, the quadrivium (arithmetic, music, astronomy, and geometry) were part of it in both. Now if the quadrivium, with all that mathematics, had a necessary place in the education of the "gentleman" and of the "scholar" in the Latin Middle Ages, the age of Albertus Magnus and Thomas Aquinas, it should be axiomatic for both the "gentleman" and the "scholar" that a sophisticated understanding of the twentieth century, the age of Albert Einstein and of Whitehead and Russell's *Principia Mathematica*, must include some firsthand knowledge of the modality of thought derived from mathematics.

In addition to what general education brings to the formation of the scholar as "gentleman," it can also contribute in several important areas to the making of the scholar as such. One such area, which we have discussed briefly earlier, is the undergraduate "major." At the very outset, it is essential to recognize how deeply it runs contrary to the prevailing attitude of many graduate professors—and, consequently, to the admissions policies of many graduate programs—to urge that the undergraduate major should be less of a miniature graduate program than it is, even for the undergraduate whose formal schooling ends with the bachelor's degree. It is more difficult still to suggest that the major should avoid becoming an imitation of the Ph.D. in the case of the student who is going on to graduate school. In many of the natural and social sciences, and no less in areas of the humanities dealing with large bodies of literary or historical materials or with difficult languages, it is almost irresistible to look for those applicants who already have a headstart in the discipline, although this may have been at the expense of general education. Why should the graduate school deny admission to students with such a headstart in order to admit students who will have to learn calculus or Greek after they land in graduate school? There is no assurance that a student who has worked in other fields will write a better dissertation than someone whose "tunnel vision" has been focusing on the field since the middle teens. Word of this preference for early specialization spreads to undergraduate campuses and then on to secondary schools, with the result that some students intent on graduate school begin to concentrate on their chosen fields in such a way as to become desirable applicants to Ph.D. programs. Thus they are, as social scientists correctly remind us, "preselected."

Yet if the graduate school insists on playing it safe by admitting students to its Ph.D. programs only from this "preselected" company, it may thereby exclude some of those with both "imaginativeness and a critical temper"[13] who most ought to become scholars. If there are to be fewer Ph.D.'s in the next generation, then let them be the ones with this imaginativeness and critical temper. The senior year of college itself is sometimes too early to demand of the potential scholar a solemn and irrevocable vow of perpetual fidelity to one particular discipline. Therefore the case for the conventional major, chosen in American colleges after the sophomore year (thus roughly at the same point at which the German student goes through the rite of passage from the *Gymnasium* to the university and preparation for the doctorate), ought to rest principally on its importance as a summation and a climax for undergraduate study rather than, as it often does now, on the foundation it supposedly lays for graduate study. It is possible—and urgently necessary—as part of any fundamental review of undergraduate education to make a case for the major as a needed focus for the learning of the college years; but as a preparation for advanced study, the major is at best ambiguous.

One reason for the ambiguity is the well-known phenomenon of the increasingly interdisciplinary character of scholarly research. A direct educational corollary of this phenomenon is the suggestion that the best undergraduate major may well be the other partner in the interdisciplinary conversation rather than the partner in which one proposes to concentrate in graduate school. Such a suggestion applies, obviously, in the natural sciences, where scholars are frequently being appointed today to fields that did not even exist when they were taking their Ph.D.'s. If graduate education is to be in the position of the quarterback—defined by one of its outstanding practitioners as "having to throw the ball to where the receiver ain't"—an interdisciplinary major may be the only way to prepare the young scientist. But it may be useful to consider the appropriateness of the interdisciplinary major in the humanities as well. If, for example, the Department of English, facing the crisis we have outlined in Chapter II, concludes that for the shrinking number of places in its Ph.D. program it should accept only applicants whose undergraduate programs have been a clear anticipation of graduate study in the Department of English, it might deny admission to some of the very students it ought most to be seeking out. Until well into the nineteenth century, after all, most of the authors with whom a graduate program in English deals were, as we would say in the modern college, "Classics majors," not English majors at all: many of them probably knew Virgil and Homer better than they knew *Beowulf* and Chaucer, or the King James Bible better than its contemporary, the plays of Shakespeare. Yet it does not seem unlikely that by now we may have some scholars-in-training in English whose first introduction to "Odysseus of many wiles" has been James Joyce rather than the *Odyssey* and who read *Paradise Lost* before they had ever read the Book of Genesis. Surely it is necessary to ask: What would happen if someone were to admit to the study of Milton and Shelley a substantial group of students whose undergraduate education parallels that of Milton and Shelley?

Yet there is need to be even more experimental than that, for modern study of human experience has opened up resources that may provide new entree to the understanding of many questions of research in many fields. As the dominant figure in that study reached over from the School of Medicine to the Department of Classics for the key paradigm of his insight into the structure and development of the human personality, so now, by scholarly reciprocity, research into literature draws upon Freudian insights and categories. Senior scholars in literature, many of whom brought from their college and graduate education little or no previous knowledge even of elementary psychoanalysis (presumably because they were obliged by their mentors to become English majors), are now acquiring such knowledge as part of their "retooling"; and they are looking for graduate students who have had the foresight to acquire some of it in college. Hence it may well be that the tortoise who has spent the college years acquiring a general education will (and should) beat out the hare who specialized too soon. These resources lead in other directions as well. Economists have sometimes seemed to proceed as though the rational models they construct had an ascertainable counterpart in the world of the competitive market, where it is often not reason, but the hopes and fears of people that determine their choices. It would be a deprivation of research in economics or political science if it could not draw some students whose undergraduate work lay in psychology and the other behavioral sciences. Or, to move to the opposite direction, scholarship in political science might well be enriched by an occasional student who had concentrated principally on *Macbeth* and *Julius Caesar* in college.

It would be quixotic to expect the admissions committees of graduate departments to cross ancestral boundaries in search of that one special undergraduate who has come the long way around; for they would fear, and rightly so, that while the net might snare an occasional genius, it would certainly bring up an entire shoal of diletantes. Nor is the performance record of interdisciplinary graduate programs as reassuring on this score as one might wish, since so many of them seem to proceed on the equation: "An M.A. knowledge of one field + an M.A. knowledge of another field = a Ph.D. knowledge of the interrelation between those two fields." And therefore it is necessary to ask: Does not the graduate dean have the opportunity, and hence the obligation, to urge colleagues—perhaps even to bribe them—into a more creative admissions policy? An undergraduate dean is, in effect, chairman of an ongoing curriculum committee, while in the graduate school the departments carry this function; but at the stage of admissions, when the graduate dean does hold at least some of the purse strings, there is a moment to strike a blow for imagination and even for risk.

There may be a compromise that is intellectually and politically preferable both to the present departmental rigidity and to an admissions policy based on the inscription of the Statue of Liberty. That is the plan for a divisional admission to graduate school, together with its counterpart, a divisional major in the college. At the present time, it would appear that the area most ready for any such proposal is the biological sciences. Typically, an undergraduate intent on scholarly research in this area (when, and if, such a student has decided on science in preference to the practice of medicine) has no clear conception of the graduate options that may be available at various universities. In one way or another, biochemistry will often be such a student's field of interest, or cell biology, or perhaps neurobiology, which, as one scientist in the area acknowledges in a recent book, is "a field that is new, multidisciplinary, and without boundaries."[14] Each of these new fields is an object of research in several of the departments in the division of the biological sciences. In recognition of this situation, it has become possible to offer divisional admission to students in M.D.-Ph.D. programs, who do not have to decide until after their first year which department is to be their graduate home. There is, in principle, no reason why such divisional admission should not be extended to all students in the biological sciences, and then to at least some of the physical sciences, where, for example, the departments of astronomy and physics are, at many universities, prepared to go ahead with it immediately: for a field such as relativistic astrophysics, the universe has become a giant laboratory, and who is to say whether a scientist working in that laboratory is an astronomer or a physicist? Indeed, why would such a question be very important? The situation in the social sciences will be more difficult, as one might expect, although the achievements of such a field as social psychology in the days of George Herbert Mead half a century ago[15] give evidence of what a divisional approach to the social sciences might be able to accomplish again. In the humanities, as mentioned earlier, it would be necessary to move one step at a time toward a policy of divisional admission, but some evidence of courage by both deans and professors could make an important difference.

Any such policy aimed at the relaxation of statutory requirements for admission to graduate study would, in turn, have far-reaching implications for the idea of graduate education. The recruitment of graduate students would seek for those who have derived from their college years as much as they need for specialized graduate scholarship—no less, but not necessarily any more. It would recognize as well that in any graduate program the student's lack of preparation in the graduate discipline is easier to repair than is a neglect of general education. And graduate programs would let it be known that they are hospitable to a select number of applicants whose general education is in better condition than is their specialized preparation. The appropriate response of the colleges to any such change of policy in the direction of divisional admission would appear to be the creation of more divisional majors. Any undergraduate major should provide the opportunity for disciplined research, to give the student a taste of participating in the expansion of scholarship rather than merely receiving the results of such expansion; for in many ways the process is more important than the results. But a major that would break out of departmental boundaries might often do this better than the conventional departmental major does, while being at the same time more integrally related to the goal of general education. Such a broadening of the undergraduate major would also be of service to those college students who do not go on to professional school or graduate school, for it would give them a more comprehensive sense of human knowledge and experience, one that would fit them for a life rather than a livelihood.

Many of the issues raised here involve the undergraduate mission of the college no less than the research mission of the graduate school. But if, as noted earlier, the graduate school has had thrust upon it the crucial role of custodian of scholarly quality and guardian of specialized excellence, its acceptance of the thesis that the products of the college must be "gentlemen" as well as "scholars" will go a long way toward liberating the teachers of undergraduates (including those who are at the same time research scholars) from the onus of having to replicate, or even anticipate, the Ph.D. curriculum in the college. There is considerable reason to believe that what holds undergraduate deans and undergraduate faculties back from a more imaginative reconstruction of their curriculum is the fear that it would put their products at a disadvantage in application to graduate school, and that the retrenchments at the graduate level today are making them even more conservative. Therefore, an aggressive policy by those charged with graduate responsibility may well open the way to a redefinition of the idea of the university that will strengthen both the general education in the college and the preparation of scholars in the graduate school.

IV

KNOWLEDGE OR PROFESSIONAL SKILL?

THE DREARY FUTURE OF a "lost generation of scholars," as discussed in Chapter II, has expressed itself the most dramatically in the emigration of scholars into professional school, sometimes instead of graduate school, sometimes after graduate school and a trial stint of college teaching. The deans of several medical schools have reported that it would be possible to fill the entering classes of their schools with applicants who already have a Ph.D.—and in the biological sciences at that.

That pattern of emigration alone would justify an examination of the other half of the problem of "balance," namely, the similarities and differences between the kind of scholarly "knowledge" represented by the arts and sciences, specifically by the graduate school of arts and sciences, and the "professional skill" inculcated by professional schools (which in the present-day setting usually means schools of law, medicine, and business).[1] An additional factor, however, is the discovery that the content of the research sponsored by the graduate school and the subject matter of the training offered by the professional school overlap considerably, and will do so increasingly. The discovery may come as something of a surprise on both sides, for this intellectual and scholarly overlapping is not currently being reflected in a corresponding integration of academic activities. The distinctive needs of professional schools deserve, and require, more attention in their own right than we are able to give them in the present essay. But professional schools and graduate schools do have much in common, including their dependence on the colleges for the general education upon which their training must build.

For an analysis of the relation between "knowledge" and "professional skill," as for an examination of general education, it is once again Newman's *Idea of a University* that contains the classic presentation of the subject: Discourse VII in the present form of the book, originally numbered "VI," takes up, to use the original formulation, "Philosophical Knowledge in Relation to Professional," which finally became what we now have as "Knowledge and Professional Skill."[2] It must be acknowledged that, even in its revised form, Discourse VII is quite disappointing. It is poorly organized, principally because it is so heavily polemical and because the author has fallen into the familiar rhetorical trap of permitting the position he is attacking to determine not only the ground of the battle, but the very outline of the discussion.[3] During 1808 and 1809, the *Edinburgh Review* had published three articles critical of university education at Oxford and Cambridge on the grounds of its lack of practical significance, and it had proposed as an antidote the utilitarian reconstruction of institutions of higher learning. These articles evoked a defensive response from Edward Copleston, Fellow of Oriel College and Newman's mentor, under the title *Reply to the Calumnies of the "Edinburgh Review,"* published in 1810. Soon there appeared the following bit of doggerel:[4]

> Since the cold cutting gibes of that Northern Review
> Have tormented and teased Uncle Toby and you,
> I'm exceedingly happy in sending you down
> A defence, which is making much noise in town,
> Of all our old learning and fame immemorial
> Which is said to be writ by a Fellow of Oriel.

Newman's chapter is a replay of that controversy—runs, hits, and errors. But whenever he does achieve some objectivity by disentangling his exposition from the acrimony of the dispute, he succeeds in setting forth several cogent points. The heart of his argument is a distinction between the kind of professional training that would be offered independently of a university and the kind that would be proper in a university setting:[5]

> There will be this distinction as regards a Professor of Law, or of Medicine, or of Geology, or of Political Economy, in a University and out of it, that out of a University he is in danger of being absorbed and narrowed by his pursuit, and of giving Lectures which are the Lectures of nothing more than a lawyer, physician, geologist, or political economist; whereas in a University he will just know where he and his science stand, he has come to it, as it were, from a height, he has taken a survey of all knowledge, he is kept from extravagance by the very rivalry of other studies, he has gained from them a special illumination and largeness of mind and freedom and self-possession, and he treats his own in consequence with a philosophy and a resource, which belongs not to the study itself, but to his liberal education.

That statement of the distinction between professional education inside and outside a university rests on the even more fundamental distinction between liberal education and professional skill, as the closing words of the quotation and the title of the Discourse indicate. In Newman's mind, "a liberal education is truly and fully a useful, though it be not a professional, education," meaning by "useful" here that which "tends to good, or is the instrument of good."[6] His reference to education as an "instrument of good" raises the question of the moral dimension in education, to which we must turn in the next chapter. But when applied to the issues with which this chapter and the preceding one are concerned, the case for liberal education that Newman was advancing was based on the assumption that only the person who is reflective both about the tasks of a profession and about its intellectual presuppositions and its philosophical implications should be trusted with the practice of that profession. Whatever may be the case with an individual practitioner, a professional school within a university must, in Newman's eyes, be committed to such an assumption. Newman was, in effect, raising the question for any university, then or now: Are the professional schools *in* the university and *of* the university, or only *at* the university? And if they were not there, would anyone—in the professional school itself or in the faculty of arts and sciences—notice the difference?

Yet in the present state of the university it is impossible for us to adopt Newman's distinction in its entirety, because of several fundamental differences between what he describes in *The Idea of a University* and our situation. One such difference is that Newman did not pay attention here to the role of research in the work of the professor in a professional school; but in many university professional schools today the demand for research as a condition of the appointment and promotion of faculty is at least as rigorous as it is in the arts and sciences, and sometimes it is more rigorous. The reason for this lack in Newman's perspective, as noted already in Chapter I, is that Newman did not pay much attention to research by professors in the faculty of arts and sciences, either. In Discourse IV he protested against the dangers of specialization "in matters of research and speculation." For him a specialist was, he said, "a man of one idea; which properly means a man of one science."[7] On the other hand, he did provide "a most significant corrective to the Dublin *Discourses*"[8] in another book, entitled *My Campaign in Ireland*, as well as in the concrete organization of his new Irish University. And, particularly in medicine, he did place an emphasis on original research also by professors in professional schools, despite the inadequacy of *The Idea of a University* on this issue.[9]

Newman's disparagement of professional preparation as somehow "illiberal" is, however, deficient as well in its failure to recognize the liberal learning that can go on in the classrooms and studies of a professional school. For the professional school must not be permitted to concentrate only on inculcating the skills of the profession, much less the tricks of the trade; nor may it simply summarize and transmit the present state of the art as this is understood by its professional guild. As this is true of a professional school that stands on its own feet, so it applies *a fortiori* to the professional school within the university. Nevertheless, there is a fundamental paradox in the situation. Because, in Whitehead's epigram, "necessary technical excellence can only be acquired by a training which is apt to damage those energies of mind which should direct the technical skill," the professional schools of a university should, in preparing students for a career, devote themselves to "promoting the imaginative consideration of the various general principles underlying that career."[10] It is in recognition of this distinctive function that Edward H. Levi has stated that, "viewed in terms of its larger responsibilities, the professional school inherits and exemplifies much of the disappearing tradition of the liberal arts college."[11] Particularly because, as we have seen, the direction of the intellectual interest within the faculty of arts and sciences tends to be dictated by the issues that are, at the moment, dominating scholarly research in various fields, it has sometimes been the professional school that has counterbalanced such scholarly overemphasis by keeping alive both study and teaching in other vital areas that do not happen just now to be on the research frontier.

A good example is the situation on the border between medicine and the biological sciences, where, as we have had occasion to point out several times, many of the most intriguing problems of the relation between graduate education and other parts of the university arise. Graduate programs in biochemistry continue to be based in medical and dental schools as well as in faculties of arts and sciences, even though, by the most recent count, the latter arrangement is more prevalent than the former.[12] The explosion of fundamental discoveries in microbiology and biochemistry during the last generation has tended to overshadow what is sometimes called, with a slightly patronizing tone, "classical biology," the study of whole organisms, of their structure and behavior. That includes the study of the organism we know best, or certainly care most about, whose gross anatomy is now being taught, at some medical schools, not any longer by the scientists in the Department of Anatomy, but by the practitioners in the Department of Surgery.

Within the total structure of the university, such a distribution of responsibilities may prove to be ultimately unacceptable. For not coincidentally, it is often the study of whole organisms that contributes most to liberal learning, as distinct from specialization, in the biological sciences, particularly for those undergraduates whose concentration falls into other fields. If, therefore, the faculty of a professional school are to see themselves as belonging to the university as a total entity, not simply to one fiefdom among many, there must be a way to involve them in the total enterprise. The independent source of funding for medical faculty, which academic administrators have welcomed for short-range reasons because it relieves them of paying the bills of the medical school, is a national policy that has proved to be deleterious in many ways; for it can deprive the university and its responsible officers of the "handle" they need to make the medical faculty recognize that they belong to the university. It is, after all, the university that gives all professors, even professors of medicine, their tenure, and it is the university, not the recipient of any individual grant, that admits students to graduate school. Reluctant though some medical school professors (and other grant recipients) may be to accept this reality, there are ways for the officers of the university, including the graduate dean, to remind them of the way things are. One such way, certainly extreme but occasionally necessary, might be for the graduate dean to turn off admissions for a year until everyone in a particular department recognizes the facts. Short of such extreme measures, the president of the university must find ways to make it clear that there is not one president for the arts and sciences, and another for medicine and the professional schools, but that the teaching and research of those schools is taking place within the one university over which this one president presides.

An authentic and meaningful "balance" would seem to demand some basic reorganization of the structure of the university. It would call for the three modalities of university education—undergraduate, graduate, and professional—to be related to one another on a divisional basis, through faculty appointments and through programs of instruction and research, with each professional school related symbiotically to one (or more) of the divisions. There does not appear to be any reason, except for the powerful reason of academic inertia, why such a rearrangement is impossible. The biological sciences today are a special case, as we have suggested several times. At several universities, where the department of biochemistry is located partly or even entirely in the school of medicine, that department nevertheless has responsibility not only for equipping physicians in the scientific fundamentals of their profession and also for the training of scientists at the Ph.D. level, but for undergraduate instruction in the field. Some such threefold structure would protect both research and teaching against sterility, as Abraham Flexner already saw when he urged that "anatomy and physiology, [as] ultimately biological sciences," could be "properly cultivated only in the university in their entirety and in close association with contiguous, contributory, or overlapping sciences."[13] On the other hand, academic history has repeatedly confirmed

H. Richard Niebuhr's warning about professional schools that "proximity to a university, even organizational connection with one, does not guarantee that this interchange will take place."[14]

Perhaps even more fundamentally, the scholarly research of the graduate school is enriched by the presence of professional schools in the same university. For a professional school can play a mediating role, by bringing into the life and thought of the university the problems that arise in its profession. Most of these problems will have an intellectual affinity with questions that are being addressed by the research and teaching of the college and the graduate school. Where there is no such intellectual affinity, that lack may itself be the object of significant inquiry, which can contribute to a reconsideration of what is going on in various locations. In addition, if the graduate school does not have a continuing association, and a continuing rivalry, with those portions of the university that are devoted to the preparation of postbaccalaureate students for the professions as well as for scholarly research, there is a danger of misunderstanding, or even of distorting, the total mission of the university. For then the graduate school will be engaged in answering questions that no one is asking any more.

Historically, the intellectual dominance of the graduate school in the modern American university—which, as Chapter I has noted, is a phenomenon of this century[15]—has its counterpart in the dominance of the professional schools at earlier stages of the history of the university. Thus Francis Bacon complained: "Amongst so many great foundations of colleges in Europe, I find strange that they are all dedicated to professions, and none left free to arts and sciences at large."[16] And it is instructive to remember that one of the seminal statements of the twentieth century in America on university education, Alfred North Whitehead's essay on "Universities and their Function," now included as a central chapter in his *Aims of Education*, was originally prepared as a dedicatory lecture for the opening of the Harvard Business School in 1928. In it Whitehead observes, with historical accuracy as well as educational sagacity, "At no time have universities been restricted to pure abstract learning. . . . The justification for a university is that it preserves the connection between knowledge and the zest of life, by uniting the young and the old in the imaginative consideration of learning."[17] In the words of an axiom from the fourth-century church father, Gregory of Nazianzus, whom Newman the scholar admired both for his "diversified accomplishments" and for the "refinement of his character,"[18] "practice is the basis of theory."[19]

A discussion of these issues at any university will inevitably lead to the question: If indeed (as we have been arguing from the very beginning of this essay) "scholarly research defines the nature of the university," which professional schools are compatible with that definition of the university, and, then more specifically, which belong in this or that particular university? The obvious negative answer is: not necessarily the several professional schools that the accidents of history have deposited there. And the positive (and more problematical) corollary would be: those professional schools that can be "liberal" (in the sense in which we have been using the term) and that can therefore contribute to, and benefit from, the treatment of their subject matter in the scholarly research that defines the university in its graduate and undergraduate colleges. For any university that is heavily committed to professional education, a review of this sort would seem to be very high on the list of priorities. Yet only a few officers of only a few universities appear to have summoned the courage to ask about what may be called (with apologies to Hans Christian Andersen) "the emperor's *old* clothes." Those will not be the same for all universities. As Newman already discovered, the organization into four faculties inherited from the medieval university—philosophy, law, medicine, and divinity—did not suit the needs of his time.[20]

Most of the growth of the modern university has been in

what the medieval university knew as the "philosophical faculty," of which the graduate school is the heir (hence the nomenclature "Doctor of Philosophy"). The growth of the faculty of medicine in the modern university has been, in effect, an expansion of scientific research into human biology, which, regardless of where it may be situated geographically or administratively within the university, is intellectually the province of the graduate school of arts and sciences in the biological sciences as a whole. Meanwhile, not only have new sciences come into being; so have new professions, and new professional schools.[21] What Newman spoke of as "political economy"[22] has now become not only political science and economics—departments which, despite their kinship, have, for reasons known best to them, elected to go their separate ways—but also, and perhaps especially, business administration. Thus the decision about which professional schools belong in a particular university depends on a clear assessment of what the needs are, but also of what that university, specifically in its graduate scholarship, does best. One method, a bit drastic perhaps but effective in its impact, would be to put the question: "If the bubonic plague were to strike this university tonight and wipe out the entire faculty (save for me and thee and the endowment), would we, after burying our dead, proceed to replicate all the hundreds of undergraduate courses and the fifty graduate programs and the dozen or so professional schools that happen to be here now?" And if the answer is obviously in the negative, then we must realize that, in a far less drastic and dramatic (and also far less convenient) way, this is precisely what every university is doing now, one faculty appointment at a time.

Although it is in many ways a well-kept secret, there is within all universities a considerable amount of such joint exploration going on in various of the fields of the arts and sciences that abut the curricula of various professional schools. Yet there remains, for example, "a great gulf fixed" at many universities between the law school faculty and the graduate school faculty, demonstrating that Niebuhr's reminder does not apply only to divinity schools. The fault seems to lie on both sides. While Robert Stevens foresaw in 1970 the emergence of some schools of law where "research . . . uses and teaches law in the framework of the social sciences and humanities,"[23] that framework does not seem to become explicit very often. Yet, whenever a verdict of "not guilty by reason of insanity" at some trial provokes widespread public discussion of the so-called McNaghten Rules of 1843, it becomes clear that neither criminal law nor abnormal psychology nor clinical psychiatry can resolve such theoretical and practical issues in scholarly isolation from one another.

A less controversial problem politically, but one that is intellectually no less provocative, is legal hermeneutics. Jurisprudence shares with literary criticism, with theology, and with other disciplines the task of trying to make sense of ancient texts in a manner that combines historical honesty with contemporary understanding. Yet even though each of these disciplines has long attempted to perform this task by reference to philosophical categories, and even though all of them are now attempting to come to terms with psychological categories, there has been remarkably little joint research into the similarities and differences between them. Perhaps those professors, whatever their individual discipline may be, who recognize the need for cooperation should announce that they will designate certain slots in their programs for graduate students who are prepared to cope with source materials of their discipline in this combined manner.

The tension between research "knowledge" and training for "professional skill" becomes particularly acute when we turn to those professions that deal in one way or another with healing—medicine and dentistry, nursing, religious ministry, social work, and others. Development by the federal government of "capitation grants" to tie the amount of support of medical research to the production of professionals who will offer "primary health care" is the most highly publicized attempt to deal with that tension. Older "training grants" for graduate students in the medically related biological sciences were in many instances replaced by "national research service awards," providing for a "payback" in the form of service after graduation. Such governmental decisions have their counterpart in legislation by various churches to keep the teaching of academic theology in their seminaries more closely related to the preparation of parish clergy. While there is undoubtedly an element of anti-intellectualism in many regulations of this sort, they also express a serious recognition of the legitimate claims of a profession and of its constituency on the educational institutions charged with a responsibility for preparing practitioners, even in a university whose very definition of scholarship has been prescribed by the graduate school.

Newman's dichotomy between "knowledge" and "professional skill," whatever its validity may be in either direction, calls attention to the deeper meaning of "profession" as *technē*, in the way that the educational ideal of the Greeks understood it. As Werner Jaeger defines it, "*technē* differs from *theoria* ('pure knowledge') by being always connected with practice," but it "connotes the practice of a vocation or profession based not merely on routine experience but on general rules and fixed knowledge."[24] It must be recognized, moreover, that the disciplines of the arts and sciences are themselves *technai* in this sense and are becoming increasingly so. As Robert Maynard Hutchins said in his inaugural address in 1929, "The graduate schools of arts, literature, and science are, of course, in large part professional schools";[25] the Modern Language Association and the American Historical Association sometimes call themselves "professional societies" as well as "learned societies." Thus the dichotomy that Newman took for granted in the title of Discourse VII of *The Idea of a University* continues to require fundamental reconsideration on all sides.

V

BEYOND COMPETENCE: INTEGRITY?

THE ESSENTIAL GOAL OF graduate education is competence in research and scholarship. Generations of graduate students have had to discover over and over that they were expected to sacrifice everything else to that goal—financial security, social life, even personal fulfillment. Everything else that the graduate school of a university does must likewise be subordinate to the demands of scholarship. Difficult though it may be to say so in the face of an oversupply of Ph.D.'s, even the training of college teachers must take second place to this task. It is, moreover, as we have seen in Chapter I, part of the primary vocation of the graduate school to uphold the standard of competence in scholarly research (howsoever defined) for the rest of the university. Recognition of that vocation has led in many universities to the designation of the dean of the graduate school as an ex officio member, or even as chairman, of the faculty committee on appointments and promotions, so that no one is appointed to a faculty position, junior or senior, in the undergraduate college or in any of the professional schools of the university without at least some consideration of the credentials of scholarship as evidenced in work that has been reviewed by peers in the field elsewhere.

This was the scholarly ideal embodied in, among others, Adolf von Harnack, "the bearer of German scholarship," for whom, as one of his admirers, Nathan Söderblom of Sweden (himself a Nobel laureate), put it in a formula, scholarship was "a higher form of life itself, not simply a way to 'results.'"[1] Nevertheless, in 1914 this prince among scholars, himself the director of the Prussian Royal Library—with his international, indeed cosmopolitan network of friends, colleagues, and former students—was able to join other German intellectuals in issuing a public statement of support for the "Ideas of 1914," defining as purely defensive the German invasion of Belgium, when the great library of the University of Louvain was destroyed by fire.[2] Shocking as such scholarly blindness during World War I may seem, it fades into insignificance before the events of World War II and their significance for the moral status of scholarship. As an earlier Carnegie Essay has summarized that significance, "World War II had been a profound intellectual and spiritual shock to many academics. Germany, that great center of scholarship, had spawned the barbarities of Nazism. Buchenwald and Auschwitz seemed to mock decades of lofty rhetoric about education's ennobling and civilizing power."[3]

A recent scholarly monograph has examined this crisis as it affected one scientific cohort, the German community of physicists. The ideology of National Socialism concocted its own definition of what scholarship, in science no less than in the humanities, was to mean in the New Order; it was formulated in all its crude simplicity by Philipp Lenard: "In reality scholarship—like everything else brought forth by men—is conditioned by race and blood."[4] Thus the university culture that had developed the Ph.D. and had defined its standards for America and for the entire scholarly world once again capitulated to a political regime which most scholars, including those who elected to stay in Germany, found morally repugnant. Of the German scholars who emigrated in the 1930s, a large number, perhaps even a majority, had ancestors or spouses not acceptable to Nazi racism.[5] Of those who did not emigrate, some preferred to remain and to voice their protest from within the university system, and others voiced no protest at all.

American scholars may be tempted to feel self-righteous by contrast; for on many of the most notorious political (and moral) issues of the past several decades—symbolized by such code names as "McCarthyism," "Vietnam," and "Watergate"—a majority of the Americans who hold the Ph.D. were probably on the "right" side. Yet some conservative critics of the academy do put the question of how much of this moral stance was due to the political atmosphere and to the liberal political orientation of so many American professors, who found it natural to oppose these three political phenomena on political grounds, and therefore how they would have responded (or did respond) to the moral implications of a political position near the other end of the ideological spectrum. Such a criticism is in many ways quite unfair, for it overlooks the storm of indignation among American academic liberals over the revelations of the atrocities perpetrated in the Stalinist era; nevertheless, it does raise, for "conservatives" no less than for "liberals," some profound and disturbing questions about the relation between political, intellectual, and moral values.

Although this essay has been affirming the definition of the Ph.D. as the recognition of no more and no less than scholarly competence, it does seem clear that in the understanding of the moral responsibility of the scholar it is necessary to go beyond competence, as well as beyond politics, to those qualities of mind and spirit that form character and conscience and that shape integrity. The relation between competence and integrity was a problem over which Newman anguished in his educational and theological thought.[6] "The scorn and hatred which a cultivated mind feels for some kinds of vice, and the utter disgust and profound humiliation which may come over it, if it should happen in any degree to be betrayed into them" were, he said, "in a certain sense true," though "essentially superficial" because they did not involve the full nature of conscience.[7] On the assumption of a certain philosophical continuity between the moral virtues and the scholarly and intellectual virtues represented by the Ph.D., the mores and traditions of scholarship have been based on a definition of integrity and character of which the "gentleman," as discussed in Chapter III, has been the epitome. It was, quite simply, unacceptable morally to cheat or to exploit or to take unfair advantage.

A test case of the problem is scholarly ambition. As Harriet Zuckerman's investigations document, it has been the ambition for recognition or for knowledge or for power that has carried many scholars from conventional to distinguished performance in research.[8] Yet from their own experience most scientists and scholars would be able to provide anecdotal evidence of a scholarly ambition that has gone beyond acceptable boundaries. The moral line is not easy to draw, but it is not impossible to draw, either. And unless scholars recognize that such a moral line must be drawn, they betray a sacred trust by failing to identify the ultimate implications of their own standards for the research in which they engage, whether as junior or as senior investigators. Whether or not it was valid in the past to take these standards for granted as something that a "gentleman" understood instinctively, the scholarly community has been gradually forcing itself to face the conclusion that we must now begin to make them explicit.

It would be a grave mistake to treat all of this as merely the academic equivalent of the rules of boxing laid down by the Eighth Marquess of Queensbury, or to dismiss anything other than a theological definition of conscience as no more than a matter of taste, as Newman did. What is at stake here is more than sportsmanship or etiquette, also more than theology or politics. It is the philosophical and pedagogical question of whether graduate education, in its relentless dedication to scholarly success, needs to define its goals with greater subtlety and profundity, so as to go beyond competence to integrity. The truth underlying the old chestnut among undergraduates about the honor system, that "the professors have the honor and the students have the system," has led to specific regulations governing the taking of examinations and the use of outside "help" in the preparation of undergraduate papers. College and university libraries everywhere have had to install technologically sophisticated alarm systems, at great expense, and to post notices that the theft of library materials makes the culprit liable to expulsion. It has become increasingly obvious that the graduate school, no less than the college or the library, no longer has the right (if, indeed, it ever did have the right) to presuppose that its faculty and students will bring with them a moral sense about the integrity of research as (to borrow a phrase from industry) "standard equipment, not optional at extra cost." The moral sense is not optional, but it does come at extra cost. And it is a cost that we must simply be willing to pay—or else.

The guidelines regulating experimentation with human subjects illustrate many of the issues.[9] Scholars had often defined the purpose of research as the single-minded pursuit of truth at any, or almost any, price. But during the twentieth century—partly, it is obvious, as a consequence of the Holocaust,[10] but also as a consequence of more general reflection—it has become clear that such a definition is both simplistic and dangerous, leading as it potentially does, for example, to the torture or the pharmacological manipulation of witnesses in order to obtain an abstract "truth." It would be reassuring if one could honestly say that the pressure to clarify and to enforce the standards for experiments with human subjects has originated within the universities and other research communities themselves. In fact, however, this pressure, like the demand that the universities take concrete steps to achieve greater justice in their policies of admission and appointment, has often had to come from the outside, usually from government. At the same time, the bureaucratic application (which, irresistibly, comes to be called "implementation") of these moral concerns creates its own set of problems—administrative, financial, and scholarly. It is undeniable, moreover, that such problems have deterred scientists from undertaking lines of investigation that have great potential for good. This is the source of the moral dilemma in which many serious investigators are caught.

In the context of the history of ideas, it is instructive to see the role played in any such discussion of experimentation with human subjects by prior assumptions on the part of scientists and scholars about the worth of the person. In the Judeo-Christian tradition, the term "created in the image of God" continues to define the value inhering in an individual, including the individual who is to become a participant in an experiment. But those who are not (or are no longer) prepared to be so explicit in the price tag they put on a human being often express an estimate of the inviolability of another self that causes them to be extremely cautious about the right they would give to a researcher to tamper with the self. No scholar would, presumably, be prepared to demean human subjects to the status of "mere research objects." Thus the enterprise of defining procedures for protecting the rights of human subjects, whether in the medical-biological sciences or in the behavioral sciences, emphasizes, negatively, the inadequacy of remaining with "competence" as the sole definition of scholarly achievement and, positively, the need to spell out what scholarly "integrity" means.

The programmatic implications of any such recognition are quite another matter. The same experience of scholarship under Nazi or Communist tyranny to which we owe our heightened awareness of the moral problem of scholarly integrity also shows how potentially dangerous it would be for the university to create academic star chambers that would impose other criteria than scholarly criteria for research by requiring of candidates for the Ph.D. degree a moral accounting of how they propose to use their degrees. On the contrary, we must, if anything, enforce even more strictly the definition of competence as the essential content of the doctorate. For it does seem clear that one of the reasons there are more Ph.D.'s than there should be has been the relaxation of the definition; and, conversely, one part (though not the only part) of the antidote is the insistence that, upon admission and at every stage of the student's career, there be a rigorous review, to be sure that only those who are truly competent reach the finish line.

Yet there is no ducking the issue of integrity in scholarly and scientific research.[11] For, in the words of an essay entitled "College Education and Moral Character" by Nathan M. Pusey, "the standards of the scholar, the mature scholar who at his best has also become a mature person, continue to impress us—his patience, honesty, industry, his sense of 'standard,' his humility, his vision of something better beyond the tawdry and the broken."[12] There is a fundamental moral difference between the legitimate expression of the ambition to succeed in scholarly research, about which we have been speaking positively, and the exploitation, without due credit, of an assistant's research, or the appropriation of a conclusion originally articulated, but not yet published, by a colleague or a student. The ideal of the pursuit of truth, already cited several times in this chapter, has been the traditional code of the scholar. That code is based, paradoxically, on both trust and distrust simultaneously: on the distrust of all prior assumptions, howsoever cherished they may be, that do not stand up in the light of further research; on the trust that moral and intellectual integrity will mark the research of colleagues and collaborators, as well as one's own. Such trust and distrust are, of course, not contradictory but complementary. The history of every discipline provides documentation for the medieval axiom that dwarves standing on the shoulders of giants can see farther than the giants do,[13] and each such history is also replete with the discarded hypotheses that have had to yield to the radical distrust generated by new truth. The history of cases in every discipline when the collegial trust in the integrity of scholarly research has been betrayed somehow receives less attention.

Yet such cases there have been, in the past and in the present, in science and in other disciplines, in this country and in others. Highly publicized instances of flagrant dishonesty in collaborative scientific research, particularly in the biological and medical sciences, may create the impression that fraud is a growing problem especially among natural scientists. But humanists had their "Ossian," which deceived even Goethe (but not Doctor Johnson);[14] anthropologists had their "Piltdown man," which besmirched the name even of Teilhard de Chardin;[15] and no scholarly discipline has the right to cast the first stone. (Nor, for the matter, has business, or government, or organized religion, or the press.) There do not, moreover, seem to be any reliable data to support, or on the other hand to refute, the impression that the past few decades have seen a significant increase in the percentage of such cases.

Yet surely even a few cases would be far too many, and there have been enough to compel those who are not only the scholars of the present generation, but the teachers of the next, to pay more explicit attention to the imperatives of scholarly integrity, by precept and not only by example. For the tissues of confidence are more fragile than is often supposed—of the confidence that scholars must have in one another, and of the confidence that others (students, institutions of education and research, patrons whether public or private, readers and interpreters) are entitled to be able to repose in scholars and in the integrity of their results. Therefore it is almost impossible to exaggerate the damage that can result from a breach of trust. Not only can it shatter an individual scholarly or scientific career; it can tarnish the entire cause of objective investigation and undermine the credibility of research, and, by violating the code so piously professed by scholars, can breed cynicism in those who have just decided to make scholarship their life's calling.

At the same time, the process of probing and testing, of inquiring and guessing, by which investigation moves forward, carries with it the obligation both of the "refutation" of the erroneous views in the work of others and of the "repair" of the erroneous views in one's own past work.[16] It is, indeed, not only (though principally) to share the outcome of research, but also to make possible such identification of mistakes, that the results of investigation, together with the data, are published. For the scholarly record is ultimately a written one: this is the foundation for the principle, often maligned and sometimes abused, of "publish or perish." Through their written work scholars frame their hypotheses and report the findings that advance their fields of study; through their original publications they claim priorities, ambiguous though such claims may sometimes be;[17] and through their books and articles they invite comparison and replication, undergo critical scrutiny, and achieve recognition. Collegial trust carries with it the initial presumption that errors occurring in such publications are nothing more than honest human mistakes.

It is when this presumption no longer seems warranted and when this trust begins to seem misplaced that the issue of integrity in research arises.[18] Although fraud and plagiarism, which almost everyone would identify as the cardinal violations of scholarly integrity, affect a large number of organizations—government agencies, journals, learned societies—each of which bears some measure of responsibility, it is with the impact of these violations on the community of research in the university, and above all on its recruits and novices, that we must be concerned here.

For within the university, where the emphasis is on collaboration and collegiality, there must arise a special set of responsibilities. The "apprenticeship" of graduate students to principal investigators, of which we spoke in Chapter I, and the team efforts required for effective collaboration in research must not be allowed to become a damper on integrity or an impediment to candor. The technical knowledge and skills involved in the contribution of a collaborator (occasionally, though not usually, a graduate student with some special background) may sometimes preclude an expert assessment of that collaborator's research by any other member of the group. The very polity of the university—including the power relationships that inhere in the structures it creates for teaching and research, and above all the unilateral power relationship between a student and a senior investigator—can make it nothing less than fatal to a career for a graduate student, or even a junior faculty member, to report fraud or misrepresentation. Sometimes, it seems, the connection between an actual individual investigation and the "principal investigator," as an entrepreneur with many projects and many grants going on simultaneously, may become so attenuated in the process of apprenticeship and collaboration that there appears to be no locus of responsibility left.

The university, the principal investigators, and the graduate students are all working in the framework of a system that has been developed—especially, as we have noted, since World War II—for conducting, supporting, and evaluating scholarly research. Throughout the faculty of arts and sciences, as well as in those professional schools that have chosen to define their standards on the basis of the standards of the arts and sciences, initial appointment is based on scholarly promise, to which graduate students are urged to aspire; promotion, above all promotion to tenure, puts emphasis on scholarly accomplishment; grant applications (and applicants) must pass a review process that requires comparison and invites competition. The fundamental intellectual criterion of competence and excellence underlying this system is sound. But it is a system designed to keep all scholars, be they young investigators or established figures in the field, under considerable pressure. Because the quality and impact of published work are more difficult to assess than is its total mass, this system all too easily lends itself to a simplistically quantitative method of evaluating scholarship, so that the volume of published output, which is so conveniently measurable, seems sometimes to determine the outcome of the competition.

The professors and other officers of the university have the obligation to make it clear, over and over, that they deplore and reject this method of distinguishing among scholars by counting pages. For even when this perception is inaccurate, it can distort the way apprentice scholars learn to read the rules of the game of scholarship; and, in scholars regardless of age, it has sometimes become a rationalization for breaches of integrity in research. It can create the assumption, in junior and senior scholars alike, that there is some sort of direct correlation between the amount of genuine knowledge gained and the number of papers published, an assumption that can encourage a rush to print. Particularly in the young and impressionable, for whom the desire to succeed may be irresistible and the competitive pressure overwhelming, this can set a pattern of the intellectual life in which intellectual rashness, scholarly slovenliness, and even fraud and plagiarism prevail over the moral and intellectual virtues of honesty and integrity in research.

Alien though it may be to the sensibilities of an entire generation of scholars, the conclusion appears inescapable that the intellectual virtue of integrity in scholarly research—which, like other articles of moral belief, may seem to be self-evident—is a principle that must be raised to the level of conscious attention and articulate formulation. One of the most effective pedagogical tools for inculcating this virtue is the study of the history of one's own discipline, which, for a variety of reasons, ought to be a required component in the process of coming of age for every scholar or scientist. Not only can such study open up paths of inquiry that previous generations considered but did not explore; it can also, by reviewing concrete instances of those who have played the scholarly game with marked cards, provide the opportunity to examine the moral complexity of "integrity" and to put the problem into some philosophical perspective. This philosophical perspective was, at least in part, what Robert Maynard Hutchins seems to have had in mind when, with characteristic intellectual bravado, he put forward what he called a "mild suggestion," that "metaphysics might unify the modern university."[19] In his concentration on the teaching of "metaphysics," Hutchins may perhaps have underestimated how here, even more than in the case of other moral and intellectual virtues, what is caught is more important than what is taught. Any senior scholar who has, over an academic generation or more, been watching graduate students go on to become senior scholars in their own right will attest to the eerie sense of seeing scholarly idiosyncracies, some positive and some negative, some trivial and some important, recur in their research and publications, and at the same time of wondering from time to time whether some simple lessons— such as "Always verify your own footnotes!"—should not have been voiced more explicitly.

Curiously, any such consideration brings the entire discussion back to an intellectual principle and an academic home truth we have been rehearsing throughout this essay: research and teaching (if possible, undergraduate teaching) do belong together—not always for anyone, not at all for everyone, not in the same proportion for every university. To quote from Whitehead's essay yet again, "Do you want your teachers to be imaginative? Then encourage them to research. Do you want your researchers to be imaginative? Then bring them into intellectual sympathy with the young at the most eager, imaginative period of life."[20] Of course there will be times in the trajectory of any scholarly career when an intensive concentration on primary research, on the sheer mass of data (whether in the laboratory or in the library) must demand priority. Those are the times when graduate students, as junior colleagues engaged in related forms of research, may well be the only students one wants or needs, and even the only students to whom one can be of much use. But there are other times when a scholar is prepared to try out, on what is for some reason usually called a "live audience" (as distinguished, it would seem, from some other kind of audience), the conclusions of an established research pattern. It is for such times that undergraduates seem to have been designed, both because they need to participate in the "minting" rather than only in the "mining" and because they would be cheated if they had to accept the minted coinage from anyone who had not meanwhile been engaged in some part of the mining process as well.

This does not necessarily mean that the only acceptable undergraduate community is one in which professors are at the same time teaching graduate students—though it does mean, contrary to folk wisdom, that undergraduates in such a university community are not being deprived simply because the faculty must give priority to their research and to their research students. More important for our present purpose, which is the consideration of the aims of graduate education, is the realization that for its very survival scholarship does depend on the existence of such a community. It is a truism that the university is a "community of scholars," but we are usually far more explicit about what "scholars" means in that definition than about what "community" means. Yet attacks mounted by the enemies of scholarship, together with scandals perpetrated by the falsifiers of scholarship, all remind us that, in the life of the university and in the training of future scholars, community—community of labor, community of trust, but also community of integrity—is indispensable to scholarship as we know it. If indeed research and teaching are inseparable, then no less inseparable are academic freedom and academic responsibility in protecting the integrity of scholarly research, not only by vigilance for the present generation but by moral commitment for the generations still to come.

VI

ELITISM VERSUS EGALITARIANISM?

PERMEATING THE DISCUSSION of the idea of graduate education, as well as every other public issue in American life, are the competing claims of two principles, identified philosophically, but also sometimes polemically, as "egalitarian" and "elitist." Despite the rhetorical use of these terms, it is important to recall that both principles—and the profound tension between them—come from Thomas Jefferson: the axiomatic doctrine of the Declaration of Independence that all have been "created equal"; and the no less "self-evident" truth "that there is a natural aristocracy," not based on birth or wealth as earlier aristocracies were, but on "virtue and talents."[1] From the first of these principles comes the "egalitarian" drive toward equal opportunity for all, and therefore toward the elimination of any artificial barriers to the full development of the natural talents of each. From the second comes the "elitist" recognition that these natural talents are not evenly distributed among the populace and that therefore equal opportunity for all implies as well—paradoxical though this may appear—special opportunity for the talented few. Not everyone can run a four-minute mile, or master the oboe, or understand the intricacies of high energy physics. "Equal rights" cannot be taken to mean that everyone should be able to do these things, nor that if not everyone can do them no one should be allowed to do them, but that those who can do them should not be denied the opportunity to develop their talents. The polarity between egalitarianism and elitism is, therefore, a spurious distinction.[2]

It may well seem from our consideration of Newman's concept of the "gentleman" in Chapter III that elitism can become a goal in itself, to the exclusion of the doctrine of "fairness" that is implied by the egalitarian ideal. If pressed to some kind of ultimate point, that understanding of elitism can become a deterministic theory of "social Darwinism," for which a predestined quality decides the outcome of the intellectual and academic competition. On the contrary, the philosophical perspective being argued in this essay would look upon "elitism"—be it in the Olympics or in an academic competition—as the natural consequence of a process in which everyone is equal at the starting line. If, because of historic injustice or social prejudice, not everyone is equal at the starting line, we must do what we can to insure such equality. But having done so, we must also be prepared to accept the outcome of the race. Otherwise the polarity of elitism and egalitarianism becomes a part of the "natural order of creation" or of the social structure.

Perhaps nowhere is the need for transcending the polarity by coming to terms simultaneously with both Jeffersonian principles more "self-evident," and yet more complicated, than in higher education. As on so many other challenges to the democratic society, so on this one Alexis de Tocqueville saw clearly what was at stake.[3] "The more closely I consider the effects of equality upon the mind," he wrote, "the more I am convinced that the intellectual anarchy which we see around us is not, as some suppose, the natural state for democracies." Nevertheless, he also had to acknowledge, as he had said earlier, that

> in America the purely practical side of science is cultivated admirably, and trouble is taken about the theoretical side immediately necessary to application. On this side the Americans always display a clear, free, original, and creative turn of mind. But hardly anyone in the

United States devotes himself to the essentially theoretical and abstract side of human knowledge. In this the Americans carry to excess a trend which can, I think, be noticed, though in a less degree, among all democratic nations.

Tocqueville recognized in "the provisions for public education" the forces "which, from the very first, throw into clearest relief the originality of American civilization," but he went on to explain that he was referring only to primary education, since "higher education is hardly available to anybody." When applied to education, the democratic doctrine of the equality of all implied that "though mental endowments remain unequal as the Creator intended, the means of exercising them are equal."[4] But in the closing decades of the twentieth century, when it is, quite obviously, no longer true in the United States that "higher education is hardly available to anybody," it follows necessarily that the colleges and universities of the nation must exercise a major share of leadership in redeeming the pledge of equality by insisting that "the means of exercising mental endowments" truly become equally available. In doing so, they must go on striving to eliminate from their own programs of student admissions and faculty appointments the vestiges of discrimination and prejudice that still remain.[5] But at the same time they must be able to attract and hold those whose "virtue and talents" give promise of advancing the boundaries of knowledge through scholarship and research. The duty to identify and to equip potential scholars and scientists must likewise be an indispensable part of the strategy and the commitment of a society that owes its intellectual and technological wealth to the research of previous generations, but that can repay this debt only by making similar deposits for the future through research and development. If graduate education, in the name of universal opportunity for all, were to renege on this duty for fear of appearing "elitist," that would be a caricature of authentic "egalitarianism"; for it would deprive the "all" of the intellectual and moral capital in which, finally, they have gained the chance to have their just share.

At this very time, however, both quality and equality in graduate education appear to be in jeopardy. Through its evolution over the past century or so, the American Ph.D. has developed its own distinctive rationale. By requiring teachers as well as scholars to undergo the regimen of a research degree, it would give potential college teachers as appropriate a preparation for their calling as any of the alternative degrees could provide, but in the process it would also discover the critical mass of those who should go on to careers in scholarship and research. Because it is often impossible at the beginning of the graduate process to identify this critical mass, their emergence depends on the assumption that everyone receiving the Ph.D. should—in laboratory and seminar, in examinations and dissertation—acquire and demonstrate the skills of an independent investigator. Some critics of the system have urged that "a formal higher doctorate" such as the degree of Doctor of Arts for college teachers might have the effect of "streamlining the Ph.D.," and they have argued that it would succeed only if it did so.[6] As our earlier discussion proposes, however, the rationale coming out of the evolution of the Ph.D. does seem to make sense—but only as long as there are attractive opportunities open in the colleges for that majority who elect to go into undergraduate teaching. In short, the way to find real scholars is to require that all teachers be scholars in graduate school, but the only way to enforce that requirement is to have positions available for the real teachers.

Now that such positions are in short supply—and, depending on how one reads the statistics, may be in even shorter supply, as we have suggested in Chapter II—the obvious danger is that, first of all, the absolute number of those applying to graduate school after college will decline, and drastically.

And that, apparently, is what has happened. "Until 1971," according to the projections of a leading econometric analysis of graduate education, "more than half of all Ph.D.'s awarded were degrees in the . . . arts, letters, and social sciences." But the analysis continues in its next sentence with the observation: "Steadily declining graduate enrollment as well as declining Ph.D. completion coefficients, however, produce a change to the extent that after 1983 less than one-third of all Ph.D.'s are awarded in these fields."[7] Therefore the total pool of the Ph.D.'s in these fields must also suffer a sharp decline.

The decline, moreover, may be qualitative as well as quantitative. If, as we have suggested and as informed impressions if not hard statistics indicate, some of the most promising potential scholars are the very ones who are finding alternative vocations in one or another professional school—engineering for the physical scientists, medicine for the biological scientists, law and business for the social scientists and humanists—graduate education could, by what is currently called a "worst case scenario," be faced with having to accept principally those who have been unable to gain admission to a professional school. It is depressing enough to think about how this would affect the intellectual quality, not to mention the morale, of the next generation of college teachers, as those who did not (or perhaps could not) make it into law, medicine, or business. It is at least as depressing to consider what will happen to scholarly research. To put the question somewhat overdramatically, will the laboratory reports and the scholarly monographs of the year 2000 have to come from "professional school dropouts"? There may be alternative (or— who knows?—better) ways of training college teachers besides the traditional Ph.D. But even most of its severest critics would agree that the Ph.D. does remain the best way to begin the training of scientists and research scholars in all the fields of the arts and sciences.

So grim a prospect becomes more disturbing still as one

turns from issues of "quality" to those of "equality."[8] No responsible interpreter of the needs and demands of those who have been excluded from full participation in graduate education on the grounds of race or gender would suggest that the acceptance of such demands by the university should in any way imply a diminution of quality for the sake of equality. To use the currently topical epithets, any such suggestion would be racism and sexism no less repugnant than its political opposites are. It must be acknowledged (as we have observed in Chapter V with regard to experimentation involving human subjects) that in the areas of admissions and appointments, as well as in certain other ethical questions, the universities, for all their noble affirmations, have sometimes taken the actions they have largely in response to the pressure of the federal government. The most highly publicized legal cases involving the admission of members of racial minorities to postbaccalaureate study—"DeFunis" and "Bakke"—dealt, respectively, with admission to law school and to medical school.[9] There has not been a case of equal celebrity involving the application of a black or Hispanic student to graduate school. The outcome of the process, however, has surely been a commitment by the American academic community to the principle that, in graduate education no less than in professional education, it is high time to set the record straight and to appoint to faculty positions a larger number of those whom history has excluded, namely, the members of racial minorities and women.

Yet, because the social and academic conventions of previous decades had identified the humanities and certain of the less quantitative social sciences as proper fields for women bent on graduate study (on the basis of the now notorious "math anxiety"),[10] the drying up of opportunities for academic appointment above all in these very fields just at the time when there is an all but universal effort to increase the number of women on college and university faculties adds yet another bitter irony to the present situation. Similarly, although the sociological factors are quite different, black and Hispanic scholars find themselves excluded—yet again—not (or, in any event, not so overtly) for reasons of their race, but because, so they are told, all the tenured positions are filled (most of them with white male scholars) and there is no prospect for further "slots," because of declining undergraduate enrollments. If, on the other hand, the university is to face litigation every time it decides, on academically valid grounds, not to promote a woman or a member of a racial minority, this poses its own kind of threat both to quality and, more insidiously, also to equality.

What is at risk in this critical situation for both quality and equality is, ultimately, the centrality of the power of the trained mind as an intellectual and social force. "Such a power," according to Newman, "is the result of a scientific formation of mind; it is an acquired faculty of judgment, of clearsightedness, of sagacity, of wisdom, of philosophical reach of mind, and of intellectual self-possession and repose," acquired by "discipline and habit."[11] For the most valuable of all natural resources is critical intelligence, and the most important of all national products is trained intelligence. This is also, ultimately, the resource on whose presence the development of all other resources depends. It would, of course, be fallacious to claim, in a nation that has produced Thomas Alva Edison and Henry Ford, that the ingenuity and the intelligence needed for the application of critical intelligence are unattainable apart from the Ph.D. But to deal with the concerns of a society and the needs of an environment that have been as fundamentally transformed as they have by Edison's use of electricity and Ford's use of the internal combustion engine does require the insights and the discipline of the natural sciences, the social sciences, and the humanities. Considerations of technological efficiency, of social utility, and of human value all bear upon these questions. Any proposed solutions which, like many of those being most strongly advocated, ignore any of these considerations, or which treat them superficially, are bound to fail. To find solutions for the issues of the day, any society, including American society, must draw upon the knowledge and basic research received from the past. If its successors, confronting similar issues whose precise contours are not yet discernible, are to be able to have at their disposal some similar drawing accounts, those will have to be deposited now.

It has long been recognized that only graduate education can be relied upon to develop a pool of investigators and thinkers who will contribute to basic knowledge. Unless someone is prepared to assert that all the important basic research in all the arts and sciences has been completed and that in this generation and in the several to follow we need only apply these assured results to a series of practical considerations, it is impossible to justify an abandonment of basic study. Without a continuation of such study, practical application faces the constant threat of being premature and thoughtless, and eventually of becoming intellectually bankrupt. Yet the United States has, in recent years, declined steadily in the percentage of its gross national product devoted to basic research and development, even as its principal Western competitors have increased theirs.[12] Because industry has sometimes been more sensitive to this need than the academy and the government, scholarship and science could face the prospect (already a reality for some fields in some countries) that basic research would move out of the universities into such research centers as Bell Laboratories, supported by industry, where there is a clear recognition—and unequivocal support—of a research that has no immediate "payoff." And in response to the inevitable question of where the next generation of scientists in Bell Labs would be trained comes the no less inevitable answer of the need for an arrangement that bears a strong family resemblance to graduate education as we know it. Those who carry out the industrial application of the basic science, moreover, will themselves be the products of a graduate education in which basic science continues to play a strong and independent role.

In the humanities and in some of the social sciences, as we have seen, the method for producing critical scholarship has been rather different. But, for the reasons already indicated, we face in these fields the twin danger of an oversupply of teachers and an undersupply of scholars. In fields where almost everyone used the Ph.D. to obtain a teaching position, it is difficult to imagine the long-term effects upon basic scholarly research if there is a radical decline in the number, not even to mention the intellectual quality, of those deciding upon Ph.D. study. The only prospect more frightening to contemplate is the situation of a technological society that is, by its own folly and shortsightedness, bereft of critical intelligence in history, literature, and philosophy just when its own scientific progress has made this a primary need.

One part of any answer to this congeries of questions is the realization that what one study has called "The Future Market for Ph.D.'s"[13] must include other ways of employing the skills of those who are the products of graduate education. Newspaper and television coverage of science, economics, and the humanities is almost automatically assigned to men and women who have been trained in journalism, rather than to those who have acquired critical scholarly skills in these fields; and the result is sometimes all too visible. The staffs of the Congress and of federal bureaus often delegate to lawyers the analysis of complex issues involving the natural or social sciences, such as energy, without the benefit of the methods of research and the tools of analysis that have been painstakingly developed by generations of scholars in the arts and sciences. Even here, however, as in the media and in government, the contributions of humanistic scholarship need to be exploited more imaginatively. Although no one would advocate an adoption of the Central European system, in which it sometimes seems that every chief of detectives demands to be addressed as "Doctor," a consideration of the total context of graduate education must include, as it is now doing, alternatives to the traditional academic career for the Ph.D.; and the faculty of the graduate school must welcome such alternatives for their students less grudgingly than they have tended to do.[14]

Nevertheless, an essay bearing the title *Scholarship and Its Survival* is obliged to concern itself above all with those select and talented few upon whom the future of scholarly research will depend, and in this sense at least it must be unabashedly "elitist." They will not be employed in television or on the staffs of Congressional committees. Nor, for that matter, must they automatically be engaged in teaching (although it will be a grievous loss to the future if they are not). The very future of the intellectual, scholarly, and scientific life of this republic hinges on the identification, recruitment, and training of such an "elite." Both private and public agencies must find more imaginative ways to continue to provide these young men and women—as the formula goes, "regardless of race, creed, or color"—with their only natural habitat during their years of apprenticeship.

It was, therefore, an act of academic statesmanship when the Andrew W. Mellon Foundation this year created a new program of graduate fellowships, with the dual purpose (as described by its president):[15]

> to attract annually into fields of the humanities 100 to 125 of the most promising potential teacher-scholars (including a number whom discouraging conditions might otherwise deflect to law, business, or other callings) by providing three-year, competitive, portable fellowships; and to contribute thereby to the minimum flow of talent and funding needed to sustain graduate programs on which future advanced scholarly research so heavily depends.

In announcing the fellowships, the foundation candidly declared its interest in recruiting "young women and men who have a larger vision of both teaching and learning than has characterized many of the products of recent graduate education." By making its fellowships portable instead of depositing them at particular universities, it seeks to break out of the present situation, in which students will sometimes select a particular graduate program on the basis not of its quality, but of its stipend. Mellon Fellows will be able to "vote with their feet," while the universities, instead of bidding for them with stipends and teaching assistantships, will be encouraged to maintain and improve the quality of their faculties, laboratories, and libraries, so as to attract them.

The educational philosophy underlying this creative proposal is, obviously, one that is very close to the "idea of graduate education" being propounded in this essay. As we have been arguing, the profound crisis in which the universities and graduate schools are caught demonstrates the need to overhaul graduate education before it is too late. For mindless retrenchment is even more dangerous than mindless growth. We have considered a great variety of questions here—questions of principle, of policy, and of program. But beneath and beyond all those questions, the crucial questions are these: Can we simultaneously preserve quality and enhance equality, thus discrediting the antithesis between elitism and egalitarianism? Can less be more?

APPENDIX

A STATISTICAL OVERVIEW

ON THE FOLLOWING PAGES, some of the basic statistical trends in graduate education are presented in tabular form. Here are a few highlights:

Enrollment: Between 1970 and 1981 graduate enrollment increased from 900,032 to 1,101,722 (22.4 percent) nationwide. Slightly more than half of the graduate students were men. The increase of male enrollment between 1970 and 1981 is modest (.4 percent), however, while the increase in female enrollment (60 percent) has been substantial. Male graduate students are more likely to be enrolled full time than are women (Table 1).

Although total graduate enrollment increased by less than 1 percent each year between 1977 and 1981, a few disciplines enjoyed rapid growth. Graduate enrollment in engineering had an annual growth rate of 5.1 percent, and the physical sciences had a growth rate of 4 percent. Education and the humanities lost graduate enrollments (Table 2). Enrollment in programs leading to masters degrees declined by more than 10 percent in education and the humanities, and by 7.2 percent in the social sciences. Enrollment in doctoral programs declined more modestly in education and the humanities and increased in the social sciences, physical sciences, engineering, and the biological sciences. This trend may reflect, among other things, the increased expectation that professors in colleges and universities must have doctorates if they are to be members of the academic profession.

TABLE 1. Graduate enrollment by attendance status and sex: 1970, 1977, and 1981.

	1970		1977		1981	
	Number	Percent of total	Number	Percent of total	Number	Percent of total
Total	900,032	100.0	1,084,970	100.0	1,101,722	100.0
Male	569,042	63.2	596,215	55.0	571,363	51.9
Female	330,990	36.8	488,755	45.0	529,909	48.1
Total Full-time	NA		435,644	100.0	446,061	100.0
Male	NA		267,592	61.4	256,575	57.5
Female	NA		168,052	38.6	189,486	42.5
Total Part-time	NA		649,326	100.0	655,211	100.0
Male	NA		328,623	50.6	314,788	48.0
Female	NA		320,703	49.4	340,423	52.0

Source: Selected data, 1970: The National Center for Education Statistics, *Digest Education Statistics* (Washington: Government Printing Office, 1972), p. 76; 1977 *Digest of Education Statistics*, 1979, p. 88; 1981: Unpublished data, The National Center for Education Statistics, July, 1983.

Institutions: The number of institutions offering graduate degrees continues to increase (Table 3). Those offering a terminal masters degree increased from 543 in 1973 to 662 in 1981. That growth includes institutions that offer course work beyond the masters level but not for a doctorate. The number of institutions offering the doctorate increased by 3.9 percent annually, from 333 in 1973 to 452 in 1981. During the same period, the number of public institutions offering the doctorate increased from 151 to 210 (up 39 percent), and the number of private institutions offering the doctorate increased from 182 to 242 (33 percent).

Graduate schools offering professional degrees increased from 78 in 1973 to 93 by 1981. A substantial majority (87.1 percent) of these institutions are private (Table 3).

TABLE 2. Graduate enrollment in selected subject fields in 1981 with annual percentage change since 1977, by institution control and degree level.

	Education	Humanities	Social Sciences	Physical Sciences	Engineering	Biological Sciences
Total	169,910	76,288	175,713	60,406	61,271	97,911
	(−3.5)	(−1.4)	(2.0)	(4.0)	(5.1)	(.4)
Public	145,974	59,501	122,625	44,447	41,018	81,496
	(3.3)	(−.4)	(2.5)	(3.0)	(4.4)	(.9)
Private	23,936	16,787	52,088	15,959	20,253	16,415
	(−4.9)	(−4.6)	(.8)	(7.0)	(6.5)	(−1.9)
Ph.D.	130,366	68,592	149,440	56,702	58,326	87,528
	(−.9)	(−.01)	(3.8)	(4.6)	(5.4)	(.9)
Masters	39,544	7,696	25,273	3,704	2,945	10,383
	(−10.1)	(−10.8)	(−7.2)	(−4.0)	(−.2)	(−3.6)
Public	145,974	59,501	122,625	44,447	41,018	81,496
	(−3.3)	(−.4)	(2.5)	(3.0)	(4.4)	(.9)
Ph.D.	109,455	52,352	101,345	41,082	38,316	72,095
	(−1.2)	(1.2)	(3.8)	(3.5)	(4.8)	(1.3)
Masters	36,519	7,149	21,280	3,365	2,702	9,401
	(−8.2)	(−9.5)	(−2.9)	(−2.9)	(−.7)	(−1.9)
Private	23,936	16,787	52,088	15,959	20,253	16,415
	(−4.9)	(−4.6)	(.8)	(7.0)	(6.5)	(−1.9)
Ph.D.	20,911	16,240	48,095	15,620	20,010	15,433
	(1.0)	(−3.6)	(3.8)	(7.7)	(6.5)	(−.7)
Masters	3,025	547	3,993	339	243	982
	(−24.2)	(−22.0)	(−20.7)	(−12.1)	(5.1)	(−15.0)

Source: Computed from selected data in "Graduate Enrollment Up In Most Sciences, Down In Education," *Higher Education Daily,* August 31, 1982, p. 2; and Graduate Record Examination Board, *Report on the Council of Graduate Schools—Graduate Record Examination Board 1977-78 Survey of Graduate Enrollment: Part 2* (Princeton, New Jersey: Graduate Record Examination Board, January 1978), Table 1.

Sources of Student Support: In Table 4 are presented data on the sources of graduate student support in selected disciplines. They indicate that in all fields but education, a very substantial proportion of student support is provided by universities

TABLE 3. Number of institutions of higher education by institution contro and highest level of offering: 1973, 1977, and 1981.

	Total	2-3 Years	BA/ BS	MA/ MS	MA/ MS+	Ph.D.	Prof.	Non-Degre
1973								
Total	2,720	1,003	763	434	109	333	78	NA
Public	1,200	760	73	138	73	151	5	NA
Private	1,520	243	690	296	36	182	73	NA
1977								
Total	3,040*	1,155	758	478	139	419	91	55
Public	1,473	921	94	158	92	196	12	0
Private	1,567	234	664	320	47	223	79	55
1981								
Total	3,203*	1,275	721	523	139	452	93	50
Public	1,498	940	86	157	93	210	12	0
Private	1,705	335	635	366	46	242	81	50

* Excludes non-degree-granting institutions.

Source: Selected data, 1973: *Digest of Education Statistics: 1975* (Washington: U Government Printing Office), p. 100; 1977: *Digest of Education Statistics: 1979*, 108; 1981: The National Center for Education Statistics, *Digest of Education Statist 1982*, p. 111.

in the form of fellowships and teaching and research assistanceships. The federal government also is a significant source of support for doctoral graduate students, but its contribution exceeds the support provided by students themselves in only biology and chemistry among the subjects selected for comparison (Table 4).

TABLE 4. Primary source of support for doctoral graduate students by selected disciplines: 1978-1981.

	Federal	National Fellowship	University	Business	Self-Support	Loans	Other
Agriculture							
1978	8.9	1.5	58.1	.5	15.0	.8	15.2
1979	7.3	1.3	56.1	.4	15.7	.1	19.1
1980	6.9	1.2	55.9	.8	15.4	.3	19.5
1981	5.7	1.6	59.0	1.4	12.8	.6	18.9
Biology							
1978	32.1	.6	49.8	.5	12.9	.1	4.0
1979	30.6	.9	48.2	.4	14.5	.4	5.0
1980	29.4	.5	51.6	.9	12.8	.5	4.3
1981	29.7	.9	49.7	.9	13.5	.3	5.0
Chemistry							
1978	9.9	.6	79.2	.8	6.3	.2	3.0
1979	9.5	.5	79.0	1.6	7.2	.1	2.1
1980	11.7	.6	78.1	1.2	6.2	NA	2.2
1981	11.2	1.0	76.9	1.5	6.9	.1	2.4
Computer Science							
1978	9.1	.9	63.6	1.8	20.0	NA	4.6
1979	6.2	NA	59.8	2.6	22.7	NA	8.7
1980	7.9	1.5	64.9	4.5	16.8	.5	3.9
1981	8.7	2.3	61.9	4.1	15.1	NA	7.9
Education							
1978	8.4	.7	18.7	.5	64.2	1.7	5.8
1979	7.8	.6	19.0	.4	63.8	2.1	6.3
1980	7.4	.7	18.4	.5	64.2	2.4	6.4
1981	6.5	.7	17.8	.6	65.6	3.1	5.7
Engineering							
1978	12.2	.9	60.0	3.3	15.9	.3	7.4
1979	10.0	.6	61.8	4.8	13.9	.1	8.8
1980	12.0	.5	61.3	3.7	14.1	.3	8.1
1981	11.1	.5	63.7	3.4	12.4	.4	8.5
English							
1978	4.8	1.3	53.8	.1	36.2	.6	3.2
1979	5.7	1.6	54.9	.2	34.0	1.0	2.6
1980	3.1	2.0	55.0	NA	35.1	1.9	2.9
1981	1.9	.8	57.2	.1	35.8	1.4	2.8

TABLE 4 (cont.). Primary source of support for doctoral graduate students selected disciplines: 1978-1981.

	Federal	National Fellowship	University	Business	Self-Support	Loans	Other
Foreign language							
1978	14.2	1.5	49.7	.2	28.6	1.8	4.0
1979	9.2	1.0	55.8	.2	31.5	.3	2.0
1980	7.9	1.4	61.7	.2	26.6	.8	1.4
1981	5.5	2.0	62.8	NA	26.6	.4	2.7
History							
1978	13.9	4.0	37.8	.1	37.3	1.8	5.1
1979	9.7	5.1	40.1	.4	38.8	1.5	4.4
1980	13.8	3.7	36.3	.3	39.3	1.3	5.3
1981	8.0	3.7	39.9	.2	40.4	1.3	6.5
Mathematics							
1978	9.2	.3	65.0	1.9	16.4	.4	6.8
1979	9.2	.9	70.1	.7	14.7	.1	4.3
1980	7.7	.3	74.2	.6	12.2	.3	4.7
1981	7.8	.3	73.6	.6	11.1	.3	6.3
Professional fields							
1978	12.7	.9	29.8	1.1	46.2	1.2	8.1
1979	10.7	.6	34.1	1.8	42.4	1.3	9.1
1980	11.1	.6	33.7	1.2	45.4	.7	7.3
1981	11.4	.4	32.1	1.9	45.0	.9	8.3

Source: Selected data from the National Research Council, *Summary Report 1981 Doctorate Recipients From United States Universities* (Washington: The National Research Council, 1982), pp. 13-14.

NOTES

WHITHER GRADUATE EDUCATION?

1. George N. Shuster, "Introduction" to John Henry Newman, *The Idea of a University* (Garden City: Doubleday Image Books, 1959), p. 21.

I. COLLEGE INTO UNIVERSITY?

1. John Henry Newman, *The Idea of a University*, edited by I. T. Ker (Oxford: Clarendon Press, 1976), p. 5; Newman's italics.
2. A. Dwight Culler, *The Imperial Intellect: A Study of Newman's Educational Ideal* (New Haven: Yale University Press, 1955), p. 311, n. 37.
3. Bernard Berelson, *Graduate Education in the United States* (New York: McGraw-Hill, 1960), p. 6.
4. Edgar S. Furniss, *The Graduate School of Yale: A Brief History* (New Haven: Yale Graduate School, 1965), pp. 24–45.
5. Richard J. Storr, *The Beginnings of Graduate Education in America* (Chicago: University of Chicago Press, 1953).
6. Laurence R. Veysey, *The Emergence of the American University* (Chicago: University of Chicago Press, 1965).
7. Richard J. Storr, *Harper's University: The Beginnings* (Chicago: University of Chicago Press, 1966), pp. 154–55.
8. In William Michael Murphy and D. J. R. Bruckner, eds., *The Idea of the University of Chicago* (Chicago: University of Chicago Press, 1976), p. 348.
9. Quoted from Logan Pearsall Smith, *Unforgotten Years* (London, 1938), pp. 168–70, in James Sutherland, ed., *The Oxford Book of Literary Anecdotes* (Oxford: Oxford University Press, 1975), p. 253.

10. *The Letters of J. R. R. Tolkien*, edited by Humphrey Carpenter (Boston: Houghton Mifflin, 1981), p. 370; Tolkien's italics.
11. Daniel J. Boorstin, *The Americans: The Democratic Experience* (New York: Random House, 1973), pp. 478–81.
12. Abraham Flexner, *Universities—American, English, German* (New York: Oxford University Press, 1930).
13. Joseph Ben-David, *Centers of Learning: Britain, France, United States* (New York: McGraw-Hill, 1977), p. 22.
14. Agnes von Zahn-Harnack, *Adolf von Harnack* (2d ed.; Berlin: Walter de Gruyter, 1951), p. 409.
15. Adolf von Harnack, "Ansprachen bei der Einweihung des Neubaues des Kaiser Wilhelm-Instituts für Arbeitsphysiologie," *Aus der Werkstaat des Vollendeten* (Giessen: Alfred Töpelmann, 1930), p. 251.
16. Ernest L. Boyer and Arthur Levine, *A Quest for Common Learning* (Washington: Carnegie Foundation for the Advancement of Teaching, 1981), p. 27.
17. Joseph Ben-David, *American Higher Education: Directions Old and New* (New York: McGraw-Hill, 1971), p. 87.
18. William James, "The Ph.D. Octopus," *Harvard Monthly*, 36 (1903):1–9; see Jacques Barzun, *A Stroll with William James* (New York: Harper and Row, 1983), pp. 283–86.
19. William Clyde DeVane, *Higher Education in Twentieth-Century America* (Cambridge: Harvard University Press, 1965), p. 82.
20. Marcus W. Jernegan, "Productivity of Doctors of Philosophy in History," *American Historical Review* 33-1 (1927):1–22.
21. Jurgen Herbst, *The German Historical School in American Scholarship* (Ithaca: Cornell University Press, 1965), p. 34; see also pp. 105-107.
22. Thomas Wolfe, *Of Time and the River* (Garden City: Garden City Books, 1935), pp. 150, 419, 441.
23. Paul L. Dressel and Mary Magdala Thompson, *A Degree for College Teachers* (Berkeley: Carnegie Council on Policy Studies in Higher Education, 1978), p. 16.
24. Oliver C. Carmichael, *Graduate Education: A Critique and a Program* (New York: Harper and Row, 1961).
25. Stephen H. Spurr, *Academic Degree Structures: Innovative Approaches* (New York: McGraw-Hill, 1970), pp. 117–38.

26. Abraham Flexner, *Medical Education in the United States and Canada* (New York: Carnegie Foundation for the Advancement of Teaching, 1910), p. 26.
27. Ibid., pp. 142-55.
28. John H. Fischer, "Is There a Teacher on the Faculty?" *Harper's*, 230 (February 1965):18–28.
29. James Bryant Conant, *The Citadel of Learning* (New Haven: Yale University Press, 1956), p. 63.

II. A LOST GENERATION OF SCHOLARS?

1. John Morton Blum, *V Was for Victory: Politics and American Culture During World War II* (New York: Harcourt Brace Jovanovich, 1976), p. 337.
2. See the table, broken down by groups of fields, in Christoph von Rothkirch, *Field Disaggregated Analysis and Projections of Graduate Enrollment and Higher Degree Production*, a Report for the Carnegie Council on Policy Studies in Higher Education (October 1978), p. 14.
3. Douglas L. Adkins, *The Great American Degree Machine* (Berkeley: Carnegie Commission on Higher Education, 1975); Richard B. Freeman, *The Overeducated American* (New York: Academic Press, 1976).
4. See the "review and critique of the literature" on this topic in Roy Radner and Leonard S. Miller, eds., *Demand and Supply in U.S. Higher Education* (New York: McGraw-Hill, 1975), pp. 13–28.
5. Earl F. Cheit and Theodore E. Lobman, *Foundations and Higher Education: Grant Making from Golden Years through Steady State* (Berkeley: Carnegie Council on Policy Studies in Higher Education, 1979), p. 110.
6. Allan M. Cartter, *An Assessment of Quality in Graduate Education* (Washington: American Council on Education, 1966).
7. Allan M. Cartter, "An Overview of the Academic Labor Market" (Urbana, 1974).
8. Allan M. Cartter, *Ph.D.'s and the Academic Labor Market* (New York: McGraw-Hill, 1976), a book whose insight has been extremely helpful in the preparation of this chapter.

9. For evaluations of Cartter, see the summary in Luis Fernandez, *U.S. Faculty After the Boom: Demographic Projection to 2000* (Berkeley: Carnegie Council on Policy Studies in Higher Education, 1978), pp. 7–19.
10. "Manpower Statistics" of the American Chemical Society for 1983.
11. *Employment of Humanities Ph.D.'s: A Departure from Traditional Jobs* (Washington: National Academy of Sciences, 1980).
12. "Projections of the Population of the United States: 1977 to 2050," *Current Population Reports*, Series P–25, Number 704 (Washington, 1977).
13. *Three Thousand Futures* (San Francisco: Carnegie Council on Policy Studies in Higher Education, 1980), p. 39.
14. Fernandez, *Faculty after the Boom*, p. 7.
15. *More than Survival: Prospects for Higher Education in a Period of Uncertainty* (San Francisco: The Carnegie Foundation for the Advancement of Teaching, 1975), p. 39.
16. William G. Bowen, "Graduate Education in the Arts and Sciences: Prospects for the Future," *Report of the President* (Princeton, 1981), pp. 11–14.
17. "Report of the Commission on Graduate Education," *The University of Chicago Record*, 16–2 (3 May 1982): 176–77.
18. Bowen, "Graduate Education," p. 5, Table 1.
19. Under the dateline of Cambridge, Mass., see the *New York Times* for 16 March 1982.

III. A GENTLEMAN—AND A SCHOLAR?

1. Ernest L. Boyer and Arthur Levine, *A Quest for Common Learning* (Washington: Carnegie Foundation for the Advancement of Teaching, 1981).
2. It will be evident that I am deeply indebted here to the work of Thomas Kuhn, *The Structure of Scientific Revolutions* (2d ed.; Chicago: University of Chicago Press, 1970).
3. Newman, *Idea*, p. 174.
4. Culler, *Imperial Intellect*, pp. 189–90, 238–43.
5. Robert Burns, "The Twa Dogs. A Tale," *Poems and Songs*, ed-

ited by James Kinsley (London: Oxford University Press, 1969), p. 110; italics by Burns.

6. Winston Spencer Churchill, *Roving Commission: My Early Life* (New York: Charles Scribners' Sons, 1939), p. 17.

7. Gene I. Maeroff, *School and College: Partnerships in Education*, A Carnegie Foundation Special Report (Princeton, 1983), pp. 7–14.

8. See David S. Levine, " 'My Client Has Discussed Your Proposal to Fill the Drainage Ditch with His Partners': Legal Language," in Leonard Michaels and Christopher Ricks, eds., *The State of the Language* (Berkeley: University of California Press, 1980), pp. 400–409.

9. Jacques Barzun, *Teacher in America* (Garden City: Doubleday, 1954), p. 120.

10. Herbert B. Livesey and Gene A. Robbins, *Guide to American Graduate Schools* (2d ed.; New York: Viking Press, 1970), p. xx.

11. Herbert B. Livesey and Harold Doughty, *Guide to American Graduate Schools* (3d ed.; New York: Viking Press, 1975), p. xxi.

12. C. P. Snow, *The Two Cultures; and A Second Look* (Cambridge: Cambridge University Press, 1963), p. 11.

13. Peter Brian Medawar, *Induction and Intuition in Scientific Thought* (Philadelphia: American Philosophical Society, 1969), p. 58.

14. Gordon M. Shepherd, *Neurobiology* (New York and Oxford: Oxford University Press, 1983), p. 4.

15. George Herbert Mead, *Mind, Self, and Society* (Chicago: University of Chicago Press, 1934), published posthumously.

IV. KNOWLEDGE OR PROFESSIONAL SKILL?

1. It is still instructive to consult the entry "Profession" in the *Oxford English Dictionary* (Oxford: Oxford University Press, 1933), 8:1427–28, for orientation on this somewhat slippery concept.

2. Newman, *Idea*, pp. 134–55; and Ker, "Editor's Introduction," pp. lviii–lx.

3. For a summary of the polemical interchange, see Culler, *Imperial Intellect*, pp. 211–26.

4. Reprinted in Maisie Ward, *Young Mr. Newman* (New York: Sheed and Ward, 1948), pp. 69–70.

5. Newman, *Idea*, pp. 145–46.
6. Ibid., p. 143.
7. Ibid., p. 76.
8. Culler, *Imperial Intellect*, p. 226.
9. Fergal McGrath, *Newman's University: Idea and Reality* (London: Longman, Green, 1951), pp. 302–305.
10. Alfred North Whitehead, *The Aims of Education and Other Essays* (New York: Macmillan, 1929), p. 144.
11. Edward H. Levi, *Point of View* (Chicago, 1969), p. 39.
12. *Peterson's Guides to Graduate Study* (Princeton, 1982), 1:160.
13. Flexner, *Medical Education*, pp. 57–58.
14. H. Richard Niebuhr, *The Purpose of the Church and Its Ministry* (New York: Harper and Brothers, 1956), p. 124.
15. Ben-David, *American Higher Education*, p. 87.
16. Francis Bacon, *Of the Proficience and Advancement of Learning Divine and Humane*, Book 2, *The Works of Francis Bacon*, edited by James Spedding, Robert Leslie Ellis, and Douglas Denon Heath (London: Longman, 1857–1874), 4:285.
17. Whitehead, *Aims of Education*, pp. 137–39.
18. John Henry Newman, *The Arians of the Fourth Century* (3d ed.; London: E. Lumley, 1871), p. 392.
19. Gregory of Nazianzus, *Orations*, 4.113, *Patrologia Graeca* (Paris, 1857–1866), 35:649B.
20. On Newman's attitude to the medieval university, see Culler, *Imperial Intellect*, pp. 252–57.
21. These are well described in Earl Cheit, *The Useful Arts and the Liberal Tradition* (New York: McGraw-Hill, 1975).
22. Newman, *Idea*, pp. 83–89.
23. Robert Stevens, "Aging Mistress: The Law School in America," *Change* 2–1 (1970):41.
24. Werner Jaeger, *Paideia: the Ideals of Greek Culture*, translated by Gilbert Highet (3 vols.; New York: Oxford University Press, 1939–1944), 2:130.
25. In Murphy and Bruckner, *The Idea of the University of Chicago*, p. 370.

V. BEYOND COMPETENCE: INTEGRITY?

1. Agnes von Zahn-Harnack, *Adolf von Harnack*, p. 341.
2. Cf. Fritz Fischer, *Germany's Aims in the First World War* (New York: W. W. Norton and Company, 1967), pp. 155–73.
3. Boyer and Levine, *Common Learning*, p. 14.
4. Quoted in Alan D. Beyerchen, *Scientists under Hitler: Politics and the Physics Community in the Third Reich* (New Haven: Yale University Press, 1977), p. 131.
5. Laura Fermi, *Illustrious Immigrants: The Intellectual Migration from Europe* (2d ed.; Chicago: University of Chicago Press, 1971), pp. 15–16.
6. See McGrath, *Newman's University*, pp. 279–80.
7. Newman, *Idea*, pp. 165, 172–73; see also pp. 413–14.
8. Harriet Zuckerman, *Scientific Elite: Nobel Laureates in the United States* (New York: Free Press, 1977).
9. See the *Federal Register*, 46–16 (26 January 1981):8366–92: "Final Regulation Amending Basic HHS Policy for the Protection of Human Research Subjects."
10. Cf. Jay Katz, *Experimentation with Human Beings* (New York: Russell Sage Foundation, 1973), pp. 292–306.
11. I have, with gratitude, drawn on "To Protect the Integrity of Scholarly Research," the report of a university-wide committee I chaired at Yale.
12. Nathan M. Pusey, *The Age of the Scholar* (Cambridge: Harvard University Press, 1963), pp. 144–45.
13. See the delightful reflections of Robert K. Merton, *On the Shoulders of Giants* (New York: Free Press, 1965).
14. J. S. Smart, *James MacPherson: An Episode in Literature* (New York: AMS Press, 1973), pp. 129–62.
15. Ronald Millar, *The Piltdown Men* (New York: St. Martin's Press, 1972), pp. 232–33.
16. Peter Brian Medawar, *Induction and Intuition in Scientific Thought* (Philadelphia: American Philosophical Society, 1969), p. 41.
17. Robert K. Merton, "Priorities in Scientific Discovery," *American Sociological Review* 22 (1957):635–59.
18. See W. J. Broad, "Fraud and the Structure of Science," *Science*, 212 (1981):137–41.

19. Robert Maynard Hutchins, *Education for Freedom* (New York: Grove Press, 1963), p. 22.
20. Whitehead, *Aims of Education*, p. 146.

VI. ELITISM VERSUS EGALITARIANISM?

1. See the Jefferson Lecture for 1976 by John Hope Franklin, *Racial Equality in America* (Chicago: University of Chicago Press, 1976), pp. 12–20, for a powerful analysis.
2. I have suggested how spurious it is in my "op-ed" article, "Quality versus Equality?" in the *New York Times* for 29 March 1976.
3. Alexis de Tocqueville, *Democracy in America*, edited by J. P. Mayer and Max Lerner, translated by George Lawrence (New York: Harper and Row, 1966), pp. 616, 427.
4. Ibid., pp. 38, 48.
5. Cf. Judith A. Ramaley, *Covert Discrimination and Women in the Sciences* (Boulder: Westview Press for the AAAS, 1978), for a careful examination.
6. Spurr, *Academic Degree Structures*, p. 190.
7. Rothkirch, *Graduate Enrollment*, p. 39.
8. See the views collected in Wayne McCormack, ed., *The Bakke Decision: Implications for Higher Education Admissions* (Washington: American Council on Education, 1978).
9. See chapters 3 and 4 of Allan P. Sindler, *Bakke, DeFunis, and Minority Admissions: The Quest for Equal Opportunity* (New York: Longman, 1978), pp. 28–62.
10. Cf. Sheila Tobias and Carol Weissbrod, "Anxiety and Mathematics: An Update," *Harvard Educational Review* 50 (1980):63–70, with an extensive and helpful bibliography.
11. Newman, *Idea*, pp. 134–35.
12. See Willis H. Shapley, ed., *Research and Development* (Washington: AAAS, 1978–1979).
13. D. Wolffe and C. V. Kidd, "The Future Market for Ph.D.'s," *Science*, 173 (1971):784–93.
14. See the recent volume, *Employment of Humanities Ph.D.'s: A Departure from Traditional Jobs* (Washington: National Academy of Sciences, 1980).

15. John E. Sawyer, "Thoughts on Humanistic Scholarship and Teaching in the 1980's and 1990's," *ACLS Newsletter*, 33–1 & 2 (1982), 9.

INDEX

A Nation at Risk, 1
academic standards. *See* standards, academic
Adkins, Douglas L.: *The Great American Degree Machine*, 16, 19
admissions, graduate, 36-38, 59, 71
ambition, scholarly, research and, 56
anti-intellectualism, 52

Bacon, Francis, 48
Bell Laboratories, 74-75
Ben-David, Joseph, 7, 9
biological sciences, 36-37, 45-47, 50, 51, 60
Boorstin, Daniel J., 7
British influences on American education. *See* Europe/European
Boyer, Ernest L.: *A Quest for Common Learning* (with Arthur Levine), 25-26, 54
Burns, Robert, 27

career patterns, graduate education and, xvii-xviii, 23-24, 75-76
Carmichael, Oliver, 12
Carnegie Council on Policy Studies in Higher Education: *Three Thousand Futures*, 21

Carnegie Foundation for the Advancement of Teaching: *More Than Survival: Prospects for Higher Education in a Period of Uncertainty*, 21-22; *Quest for Common Learning, A* (Ernest L. Boyer and Arthur Levine), 25-26, 54; *Second Annual Report*, 5
Cartter, Allan M., 19
Census, United States Bureau of the, birth rate projections by the, 20-21
Churchill, Winston, 27
college(s). *See* undergraduate education; university/universities
Columbia University, 5-6
community of scholars, 65-66
competence, scholarly. *See* integrity; standards, academic
Conant, James C., 14
Copleston, Edward: *Reply to the Calumnies of the "Edinburgh Review"*, 42
Culler, A. Dwight, 26-27
culture. *See* language requirements
curriculum. *See* biological sciences; English; humanities; interdisciplinary study; language requirements; social sciences; specialization, undergraduate

dean, of graduate education, 53
demographic trends, graduate education and, 20-24
departmentalization, 50
discrimination, in higher education, 69, 72
dissertation, 9-10, 12-13, 28, 29
Doctor of Arts, 11, 70
Doctor of Philosophy. *See* Ph.D.
Dressel, Paul L., 11

Edinburgh Review, 42
editorial services, scholars need for, 29
education, higher, discrimination in, 69, 72; influences on, 6-8, 12-13, 53-54
elitism, Chapter VI *passim* (67-77); graduate education and, 70, 71-72; Newman's views on, 68; social Darwinism and, 68. *See also* discrimination
English (language), scholar's need for proficiency in, 27-29
equalitarianism. *See* elitism
Europe/European, influences on American higher education, 6-8, 12-13, 53-54; lack of practical orientation in universities of, 42. *See also* graduate education; scholar(s)/scholarship
experimentation with human subjects, 57-58

federal government, influence on universities of, 46, 51-52, 57, 72
fellowships, 76-77
Flexner, Abraham, 7, 13, 47
Freeman, Richard B.: *The Overeducated American*, 16, 19

G.I. Bill of Rights, 16
Gant, Elmer, 11
general education, humanists and, 32; language requirements and, 30-32; Newman's views on, 26-27; professional training and, 41-42; quantitative skills and, 32; scholarship and, 25-26; undergraduate education and, 12
gentleman. *See* scholar(s)/scholarship
German influences on American education. *See* Europe/European
graduate education/school(s), academic standards and, 13-14, 53; aims of, 38-39, 53, 65; career patterns and, xvii-xviii, 23-24, 75-76; dean of, 53; demographic trends and, 20-24; European influences on, 7-8, 9-10; funding of, xvii, 17, 18, 76-77; history/growth of, 5-6, 15-17; intellectual dominance of, 48; language requirements and, 29-32; studies about, 2-3; undergraduate education and, 10-11, 25, 32-35, 38-39; university presses and, 29. *See also* admissions, graduate; graduate student(s); professional training/education; reform, educational; research; scholar(s)/scholarship; university/universities
graduate student(s), 17, 18, 61-62, 65
Great American Degree Machine, The (Douglas L. Adkins), 16, 19
Gregory of Nazianzus, 49
Guide to American Graduate Schools (Livesey, Herbert B., et al.), 29

Harnack, Adolf von, 8, 53-54
Harper, William Rainey, 6
Harvard University, 5-6
health education, 51. *See also* biological sciences; professional training
honor system, 56-57
human subjects, experimentation with, 57-58
humanities/humanists, general education and the, 32; graduate admissions/education and the, 5-6, 18, 37; research integrity and scholarship in the, 60, 75; women in the, 72
Hutchins, Robert Maynard, 52, 64

Idea of a University, The. *See* Newman, John Henry
integrity, Newman's views on, 55-56; research and, 59-60; scholarship and, 60-61, 63. *See also* moral values; standards, academic
interdisciplinary study, biological sciences and, 36-37; research/scholarship and, 34-36, 50-51. *See also* admissions, graduate; biological sciences; specialization, undergraduate

Jaeger, Werner, 52
James, William, 9
Jefferson, Thomas, 67, 68
Johns Hopkins University, 5-6
Jowett, Benjamin, 6

language requirements, 29-32
Lenard, Philipp, 54
Levi, Edward H., 45

Levine, Arthur: *A Quest for Common Learning* (with Ernest L. Boyer), 25-26, 54
liberal education, Newman's views on, 43-45; professional training and, 45-46. *See also* general education; undergraduate education
Livesey, Herbert B.: *Guide to American Graduate Schools*, 29

major, undergraduate. *See* specialization, undergraduate
Mann, Lane, xviii
mathematics. *See* quantitative skills
McNaghten Rules (1843), 51
medical education. *See* biological sciences; professional education
Mellon (Andrew W.) Foundation, 76-77
moral values, Chapter V *passim* (53-66); academic standards and, 56, 59; honor system and, 56-57; Nazism and, 54, 58; Newman's views on, 56; Ph.D. and, 58-59; scholarly ambition and, 56
More Than Survival: Prospects for Higher Education in a Period of Uncertainty (Carnegie Foundation for the Advancement of Teaching), 21-22

National Academy of Sciences, 20
National Research Council. *See* National Academy of Sciences
Nazism, moral values and, 54, 58
Newman, John Henry: *Idea of a University, The*, admiration of Gregory of Nazianzus by, 49;

Newman, John Henry (*cont.*)
definition of a university by, 5; nature of the university, 3, 24; on competence and integrity, 55-56; on elitism and the concept of a gentleman, 68; on general/liberal education, 26-27, 43-45; on moral values and scholarship, 56; on organization of the faculty, 49; on professional training, 41-45, 52; on teaching/research, 14, 44; on the power of the mind, 73; *My Campaign in Ireland*, 44

Neibuhr, H. Richard, 47-48, 51

Overeducated American, The (Richard B. Freeman), 16, 19

Ph.D. (Doctor of Philosophy), as a professional degree, 9, 19; awarding of, 1, 5-6, 8-9, 11-12, 16, 19, 70, 71; commitment to, 15; definition/meaning of, 12, 55; moral values of the, 55-56, 58-59; research and the, 9-10, 11-12; supply/demand of, 19-20, 70, 75; teaching and the, 9-10, 11-12, 19-20, 70; tenure and the, 8. *See also* Doctor of Arts; professional training/education

physical sciences, graduate admissions and the, 37

politics, scholarship and, 55

presses, university, graduate education and, 29

Princeton University, 5-6

professional training/education, European influence on, 8-9; general/liberal education and, 41-42, 43-46; graduate education and, 13, Chapter IV *passim* (41-52), 71; Newman's views on, 42-45, 52; Ph.D. as a degree for, 9, 19-20; role of federal government in promotion of, 46, 51-52; scholarship/research and, 44, 52; universities and, 42-44, 45-48, 50-51. *See also* biological sciences; research

publications, scholarly, 13, 61-63

Pusey, Nathan M.: "College Education and Moral Character," 59

quantitative skills, general education and, 32

Quest for Common Learning, A (Ernest L. Boyer and Arthur Levine), 25-26, 54

reform, graduate educational, 1-2, 76-77

research, academic standards and, 62-63; as an essential aspect of the university, 6-7, 49, 62-63; definition of, 57; graduate students and, 17, 61-62, 65; interdisciplinary studies and, 50-51; Newman's views on, 14, 44; Ph.D. and, 9-10, 11-12; professional training and, 44-45; scholarly ambition and, 56; science and, 12, 17, 74-75; social issues and basic, 73-74; teaching and, 13-14, 64, 66; tenure and, 62; undergraduate education and, 12-14, 65. *See also* graduate education/

schools(s); integrity; scholar(s)/ scholarship

scholar(s)/scholarship, as a career, xvii-xviii, 23-24, 75-76; as a gentleman, Chapter III *passim* (25-39), 55-56; community of, 65-66; definition of, 12, 53-54; demands of, 53; general education and, 26-27; graduate education and, 52; humanities and, 75; integrity and, 60-61, 63; moral aspects of, Chapter V *passim* (53-66); Nazism and, 54; need for editorial services of, 29; need for proficiency in English of, 27-29; political issues and, 55; professional training and, 44, 51-52; social sciences and, 75; World War II and, 54. *See also* graduate eduation; integrity; Ph.D; research
science(s), research in the, 12, 17, 74-75. *See also* biological sciences; physical sciences; social sciences
seminars, graduate, 10, 18
Shuster, George N., 3
Snow, C. P., 32
social Darwinism, 68
social issues, basic research and, 73-75
social sciences, 18, 37, 72, 75
Söderblom, Nathan, 53-54
specialization, undergraduate, graduate education and, 32-35, 37-38. *See also* admissions, graduate; interdisciplinary study
standards, academic, 12-14, 53, 56, 59, 62. *See also* integrity; moral values

Stevens, Robert, 51
supply/demand of Ph.D.s. *See* Ph.D., supply/demand of
support of graduate students, 17

teaching, definition of a university and, 5; graduate students and, 18; Newman's views on, 14; Ph.D. and, 9-10, 11-12, 19-20, 70; research and, 12-14, 64, 66; science education and, 12; undergraduate education and, 20. *See also* Doctor of Arts
tenure, 8, 13, 62
Thompson, Mary Magdala, 11
Three Thousand Futures (Carnegie Council on Policy Studies in Higher Education), 21
Tocqueville, Alexis de, 68-69
Tolkien, J.R.R., 6
Trent, Council of, 7

undergraduate education, academic standards and, 12-14; general education and, 12; graduate education and, 10, 25; mission of, 8, 38-39; Ph.D.s and, 8-9; research and, 12-14, 65; teaching and, 20
United States Bureau of the Census. *See* Census, United States Bureau of the
university/universities, as a community of scholars, 65-66; definition/mission of, 5, 14, 15, 38-39, 48-49; federal government and, 51-52, 57, 72; history of, 7-9, 48-50; integrity, power relationships and the, 61-62; professional training and, 42-44, 45-48, 49-51; re-

university/universities (*cont.*)
search/teaching and the, 5-7, 49, 62; structure of, 47-48; undergraduate education and, 8. *See also* departmentalization; graduate education/school(s)
University of Chicago, 6
University of Pennsylvania, 5-6

Whitehead, Alfred North, 45;
"Universities and their Function," 48-49, 64
women, in higher education, 72-73
World War II, scholarship and, 54

Yale College, 5-6

Zuckerman, Harriet, 56

LIBRARY OF DAVIDSON COLLEGE

Books on regular loan may be checked out for **two weeks**. Books must be presented at the Circulation Desk in order to be renewed.

A fine is charged after date due.

Special books are subject to special regulations at the discretion of the library staff.